creating the *happiest* of HOLIDAYS

LEISURE ARTS, INC.
Little Rock, Arkansas

EDITORIAL STAFF

Editor-in-Chief: **Susan White Sullivan**
Designer Relations Director: **Debra Nettles**
Craft Publications Director: **Cheryl Johnson**
Art Publications Director: **Rhonda Shelby**
Special Projects Director: **Susan Frantz Wiles**
Senior Prepress Director: **Mark Hawkins**
Technical Editor: **Mary Sullivan Hutcheson**
Contributing Editors: **Laura Siar Holyfield,
Lois J. Long, and Jane Kenner Prather**
Contributing Test Kitchen Assistant: **Rose Glass Klein**
Editorial Writer: **Susan McManus Johnson**
Designers: **Kim Hamblin, Anne Pulliam Stocks,
Lori Wenger, and Becky Werle**
Art Category Manager: **Lora Puls**
Graphic Artist: **Amy Temple**
Production Artist: **Janie Wright**
Imaging Technicians: **Brian Hall, Stephanie Johnson,
and Mark R. Potter**
Photography Manager: **Katherine Atchison**
Contributing Photo Stylist: **Christy Myers**
Publishing Systems Administrator: **Becky Riddle**
Publishing Systems Assistants: **Clint Hanson and John Rose**

BUSINESS STAFF

Vice President and Chief Operations Officer:
Tom Siebenmorgen
Director of Finance and Administration: **Laticia Mull Dittrich**
Vice President, Sales and Marketing: **Pam Stebbins**
National Accounts Director: **Martha Adams**
Sales and Services Director: **Margaret Reinold**
Information Technology Director: **Hermine Linz**
Controller: **Francis Caple**
Vice President, Operations: **Jim Dittrich**
Comptroller, Operations: **Rob Thieme**
Retail Customer Service Manager: **Stan Raynor**
Print Production Manager: **Fred F. Pruss**

CREDITS

We want to especially thank Mark Mathews of
Mark Mathews Photography and Ken West of
Ken West Photography for their excellent work.

We would like to recognize the following
companies for providing yarn: Bernat® Yarn Company,
Patons® Yarn Company, and Lion Brand® Yarn Company.

Special thanks go to Lois J. Long for designing the Child's Hat
and to Sue Galucki for knitting the photography models.

ISBN-13: 978-1-60140-884-6 • ISBN-10: 1-60140-884-6

10 9 8 7 6 5 4 3 2 1

creating the *happiest* of HOLIDAYS

Christmas bliss is yours to create

with dozens of scrumptious recipes

and amazing gift ideas.

Give everyone your best, and make this

the *happiest* of HOLIDAYS!

Contents

creative *gift giving* for the HOLIDAYS

Something for *everyone* on your list,
including the family pet! Whether you like
to sew, paint, bead, knit, or just *craft* in general,
you'll find plenty of great ideas
for *creative gifts*.

Charm Bracelet & Bag

• link chain for bracelet (about 7" long) • wire cutters • E beads and 10mm glass beads • 1" head pins • round-nose jewelry pliers • 5mm jump rings • needle-nose jewelry pliers • charms • toggle clasp • 4 coordinating fabrics • embroidery floss • 1$1/2$" button cover kit • felt • paper-backed fusible web • scalloped pinking shears

For all sewing, match the right sides and use a $1/4$" seam allowance unless otherwise stated.

1. For the bracelet, cut the chain about $1/2$" shorter than the desired finished length.
2. For each bead dangle, thread a small and large bead on a head pin; trim the pin $1/4$" from the large bead and make an eye loop (page 142).
3. Use jump rings (page 142) to attach the charms, bead dangles, and the toggle clasp to the bracelet.
4. For the bag, cut two 5$1/2$" x 2" fabric pieces and two 5$1/2$" x 3" coordinating fabric pieces.
5. Sew 1 piece of each fabric together along 1 long edge for the bag front. Repeat to make the bag back.
6. For the side tab, match the short edges of a 4$1/2$" x 2$1/2$" fabric piece. Sew the edge opposite the fold. Turn right side out and press flat, with the seam at the center back. Matching the raw edges, fold in half and press flat.
7. For each tie, cut a 9" x 1" fabric piece. Press 1 short end $1/4$" to the wrong side. Matching the long edges, sew the tie along the long raw edge. Turn the tie right side out.
8. Matching raw edges, pin the side tab to the bag front. Sew the bag front and back together along the side and bottom edges. Clip the corners and turn right side out. Matching raw edges, pin the ties to the top edges of the bag.
9. For the lining, cut two 5$1/2$" x 4$1/2$" fabric pieces. Sew the lining together along 1 short end and 2 side edges, leaving an opening at the bottom for turning. Clip the corners. Do not turn right side out.
10. Place the bag inside the lining, making sure that the ties are in between. Sew the top edge. Turn the bag right side out and press. Sew the opening closed.
11. Draw the recipient's initials on a fabric scrap and work Stem Stitches (page 141) with 2 strands of embroidery floss. Cover the button and sew it to the bag.
12. Fuse 2 pieces of felt together and using the scalloped shears, trim to a 4" x 3$3/4$" piece. Tack the bracelet to the felt and place it in the bag.

Charm Bracelet & Bag

Pendant Key Fob

- 5mm smooth disk beads • 10mm glass beads
- 2" eye pins • needle-nose jewelry pliers • E bead
- 1" head pin • seed beads • 4x6mm faceted rondelle beads • charm • pendant • wide oval chain links
- metal key ring with attached jump ring

1. To make the first dangle, alternate 3 disk beads and two 10mm beads on an eye pin; make an eye loop at the end (page 142). Thread an E bead and a 10mm bead onto a head pin; connect the 2 pieces with eye loops.
2. For the second dangle, thread 1 seed bead and 2 rondelle beads on an eye pin; repeat twice more. Connect the pieces, placing the charm at the bottom of the dangle.
3. For the pendant dangle, join the pendant to 2 links of the chain.
4. Join the dangles to the jump ring (page 142) on the key ring.

Pendant Key Fob

Charm Necklace

- wire cutters • chain necklace with links large enough to accommodate jump rings • 4mm jump rings • decorative jewelry pin • assorted charms, jewelry pieces, and bells • 20-gauge jewelry wire
- needle-nose pliers • glass beads • 2" eye pins
- 6mm dia. beaded garland

1. Cut the chain apart at center front. Attach the cut ends to the sides of the pin with jump rings (page 142).
2. Attach the charms, jewelry pieces, and bells to the links in the chain. If the item doesn't have a hanger or opening for the jump ring, tightly wrap a length of wire around the item, forming a hanger near one end.
3. To attach beads, thread each bead on an eye pin. Loop the eye pin around the jewelry pin, jump ring, or a link in the chain.
4. Tightly wrap wire around 1 end of the beaded garland, then wrap the opposite wire end around a link in the chain next to the clasp. Wrap the beaded garland around the chain and secure the end to the opposite end of the chain. Trim the wire ends.

Charm Necklace

Amethyst Necklace

Best Friends Necklaces & Bracelets

Amethyst Necklace
- jewelry wire cutters • 7-strand silver plate nylon-coated wire • toggle clasp • crimp beads • crimping jewelry pliers • fourteen 4mm yellow jade cube beads • eighteen 4mm round amethyst beads • graduated amethyst pear-shaped beads

1. Cut a 27" wire length.
2. Attach one end of the toggle clasp to the wire with a crimp bead (page 142), leaving a 1" wire end. Thread a cube and a crimp bead onto the wires. Close the crimp bead. Trim any excess wire.
3. Skip about 1¼" and attach a crimp bead; then, add a round bead, a cube, another round bead, and finally, attach a crimp bead. Repeat this sequence 3 more times.
4. For the focal beads, skip about 1¼" again and attach a crimp bead and a round bead; then, alternate cube and pear beads. Add a round and a crimp bead to complete the focal cluster.
5. Thread beads and a clasp on the remaining half of the necklace, mirroring the first half.

Best Friends Necklaces & Bracelets
- 10mm silver ring beads
- 4x7mm pony beads • 6mm block alphabet beads • 18" day glow ball chains • 8mm plated round pearl beads • silver elastic cord • jeweler's cement

For the necklaces, string the beads on day glow ball chains. For the bracelets, string the beads on silver cords, tying the ends together with square knots. Add a drop of jeweler's cement to each knot.

Beaded Charm Watch

Sunburst Ball

• 2" dia. foam ball • silver spray paint • 2" head pins • 3mm silver round beads • 6mm white rondelle beads • 6mm crystal faceted beads • 10mm white sunburst beads • straight pins • craft glue • monofilament

1. Spray paint the ball in a well-ventilated area.
2. Load 20 head pins with 1 silver bead, 1 rondelle bead, 1 faceted bead, 1 silver bead, and 1 sunburst bead. Push the pins into the ball, spacing evenly.
3. Load 20 straight pins with 1 silver bead, 1 rondelle bead, and 1 faceted bead. Push the pins into the ball, spacing evenly.
4. Fill in the gaps with straight pins, each loaded with 1 silver bead and 1 sunburst bead.
5. Adjust the pins as desired. Remove the pins, one at a time, dip the tip into craft glue, and reinsert into the ball to secure.
6. For the hanger, loop and tie monofilament to a straight pin. Secure in the ball.

Beaded Charm Watch

• watch face • charms • jump rings • tigertail beading wire • jewelry wire cutters • assorted glass beads • crimp beads • toggle clasp • crimping jewelry pliers

1. Loosely measure around your wrist. Divide the measurement in half.
2. Thread each charm onto a jump ring (page 142).
3. Working on one side of the watch, center a 12" length of wire through one lug on the watch; then, bend it in half. Thread ³/₄" to 1" of beads and charms onto each wire, then thread both ends through one bead; repeat until the measurement determined in Step 1 is reached.
4. Thread a crimp bead and half of the toggle clasp onto one wire end. Thread the end back through the crimp bead; close the crimp bead (page 142) and trim the excess wire. Repeat with the remaining wire end.
5. Repeat Steps 3 and 4, using the remaining half of the clasp.

Large Sunburst Ball

- 3" dia. foam ball • corsage pins • 4mm white round beads
- 9mm clear silver-lined bugle beads • 25mm white sunburst beads • 8mm white opalescent round sequins • white round-headed straight pins • craft glue • monofilament

1. Load 20 corsage pins with one 4mm bead, 1 bugle bead, one 4mm bead, and 1 sunburst bead. Push the pins into the ball, spacing evenly.
2. Load 50 corsage pins with 1 bugle bead and 1 sequin. Push the pins into the ball, spacing evenly.
3. Fill in the gaps with straight pins, each loaded with 1 sequin.
4. Adjust the pins as desired. Remove the pins, one at a time, dip the tip into craft glue, and reinsert into the ball to secure.
5. For the hanger, loop and tie monofilament to a straight pin. Secure in the ball.

Small Sunburst Ball

- 1¼" dia. foam ball • silver spray paint • 2" head pins
- 3mm silver round beads
- 6mm white rondelle beads
- 6mm crystal faceted beads
- 10mm white sunburst beads
- straight pins • craft glue
- monofilament

1. Spray paint the ball in a well-ventilated area.
2. Load 7 head pins with 1 silver bead, 1 rondelle bead, 1 faceted bead, 1 silver bead, and 1 sunburst bead. Load 7 straight pins with 1 silver bead, 1 rondelle bead, and 1 faceted bead.
3. Push the loaded pins into the ball around the center, alternating pin sizes.
4. Adjust the pins as desired. Remove the pins, one at a time, dip the tip into craft glue, and reinsert into the ball to secure.
5. For the hanger, loop and tie monofilament to a straight pin. Secure in the ball.

Large Sunburst Ball (top)

Sunburst Ball (center)

Small Sunburst Ball (bottom)

Sunbonnet Sue Apron

- 15" fabric square for embroidery
- embroidery floss and embroidery needle
- embroidery hoop (optional) • 1$\frac{1}{4}$ yards of fabric for apron • 12$\frac{1}{2}$" x 10$\frac{1}{4}$" white fabric piece for lining

For all sewing, match the right sides and use a $\frac{1}{2}$" seam allowance unless otherwise stated. We used 2 strands of floss for all embroidery stitches (page 141).

1. Enlarge the patterns (page 143) to 109%. Transfer the patterns (page 142) onto the fabric square, repeating the border motif as desired. Referring to the photo and pattern, embroider the design. Trim the stitched fabric to 12$\frac{1}{2}$"w x 8$\frac{1}{2}$"h.
2. From the apron fabric, cut a 21" x 44" piece for the apron skirt, a 5" x 84" strip for the waistband tie (pieced as necessary), a 3" x 24$\frac{1}{2}$" strip for the neckband, and a 2$\frac{3}{4}$" x 12$\frac{1}{2}$" strip for the apron bib border.
3. Sew the apron bib border to the top of the embroidered piece.
4. Fold the neckband in half lengthwise; sew, leaving an opening for turning. Turn the neckband right side out, press, and sew the opening closed. Matching the ends and the top raw edge of the apron bib border, baste the neckband to the border at each upper corner.
5. Sew the lining to the bib, leaving an opening for turning at the bottom. Turn right side out, press, and sew the opening closed.
6. Press both short ends and one long edge of the apron skirt $\frac{1}{4}$" to the wrong side twice; sew. Baste $\frac{1}{2}$" and $\frac{1}{4}$" from the remaining raw edge; pull the basting threads to gather the skirt to 20".
7. Press all edges of the waistband $\frac{1}{2}$" to the wrong side. With wrong sides together, press the waistband in half lengthwise. Centering the skirt on the waistband, sandwich and pin the gathered edge of the skirt $\frac{1}{2}$" between the pressed edges of the waistband. Topstitch the waistband close to the pressed edges.
8. Pin the bib to the center of the waistband. Topstitch in place.

Sunbonnet Sue Apron

❋*13*

Daily Kitchen Towels

Garnet Pillow

Redwork Pillowcases

14

Daily Kitchen Towels

- flour sack kitchen towels
- embroidery floss and embroidery needle • embroidery hoop (optional)

Enlarge the patterns (pages 144-145) to 162%. Transfer the patterns (page 142) onto the towels. Referring to the photo and patterns, embroider (page 141) the designs. We used 1 strand of floss for the Running Stitches on Tuesday's socks and 3 strands of floss for all other stitches.

Garnet Pillow

- rectangular pillow with removable cover • embroidery floss and embroidery needle • embroidery hoop (optional)

Remove the pillow cover from the pillow. Follow Sizing Patterns (page 142) to size the pattern (page 147) to fit the pillow. Transfer the pattern (page 142) onto the pillow cover. Referring to the photo and pattern, embroider (page 141) the design. We used 3 strands of floss for all stitches.

Redwork Pillowcases

- pillowcases • embroidery floss and embroidery needle • embroidery hoop (optional) • 2 buttons

Enlarge the patterns (page 146) to 143%. Transfer the patterns (page 142) onto the pillowcases. Referring to the photo and patterns, embroider (page 141) the design. We used 3 strands of floss for all stitches. Sew a button on each pillowcase.

Bluebird

- overdyed wool felt and hand-dyed wool • 12½" muslin square • variegated embroidery floss and embroidery needle • embroidery hoop (optional) • artist's pastels • beading needle and thread • assorted beads • spray adhesive • 17" square frame with mat board

1. Enlarge the patterns (page 146) to 184%. Using the patterns, cut the beak, flowers, and leaves from wool felt or wool.
2. Transfer the remaining pattern lines (page 142) onto the muslin square. Referring to the photos and pattern, embroider (page 141) the design. We used 6 strands of floss for the bird outline, wing, and branch. We used 1 strand to Blanket Stitch the beak and leaves to the muslin and for the tail, breast, and leaf Running Stitch details.
3. Color and shade the bird and branch with the pastels. Use thread to sew the flowers and beads to the muslin.
4. Fray the edges of the muslin, spray the back with adhesive in a well-ventilated area, and press it onto the mat board. Place the mat board in the frame.

Beautiful Throw

approx finished size: 45¹/₂" x 66¹/₂"

• ¹/₂ yard each of 6 coordinating velveteen fabrics • 2¹/₈ yards of 54"w fabric for backing/binding • low-loft batting • invisible nylon thread • silk ribbon

For all sewing, match the right sides and use a ¹/₂" seam allowance unless otherwise stated. Place velveteen face down on a thick bath towel when pressing. Alternate directions when pressing seam allowances in Steps 1 & 2.

1. Cut fifty-eight 8¹/₂" squares of velveteen. Referring to Fig. 1, sew the squares together into 10 strips.
2. Sew the strips together to complete the throw top. Trim as shown (Fig. 2).
3. Cut the quilt backing fabric to 4" larger than the throw top on each side. Press ¹/₂" to the wrong side on all edges of the backing.
4. Cut 4 layers of batting 1¹/₂" larger than the throw top on each side.
5. Layer the backing (right side down), the batting layers, and the throw top (right side up). Pin all layers together at each seam intersection.
6. Fold the backing sides to the front of the throw top, covering the raw edges of the top and overlapping the top by about ¹/₂"; pin in place. Zigzag stitch the "binding" in place with the nylon thread. Repeat at the top and bottom of the throw.
7. Tie the throw with lengths of silk ribbon, making a square knot at each seam intersection.

Fig. 1

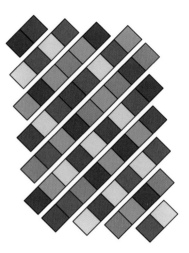

Fig. 2

Beautiful Throw

Knitting Needle Roll

Blanket in a Backpack

Knitting Needle Roll

- 21" x 34" fabric piece for the body • 21" x 23" fabric piece for the top pocket • 21" x 16" fabric piece for the bottom pocket • $5/8$ yard each of rickrack and 1"w ribbon • clear nylon thread • 21" x $16^1/2$" piece of batting • $1/3$ yard of $1^1/4$"w twill tape • large sewing snap • large button

For all sewing, use a $1/2$" seam allowance unless otherwise stated.

1. Matching the wrong sides and short ends, fold the body and top pocket pieces in half. Matching the wrong sides and long edges, fold the bottom pocket in half. Press the folds.
2. Cut a 21" length each from rickrack and ribbon. Pin the trims near the folds of the pockets; zigzag stitch with nylon thread.

3. Unfold the body wrong side up. Pin, then baste the batting to the lower half of the fabric, aligning one long edge of the batting with the fold. Leaving the piece unfolded, turn the body right side up. Aligning raw edges, layer and pin the top and bottom pockets on the lower half of the body; baste along the side and bottom edges.

4. Matching right sides, refold the body. Leaving an opening at the bottom for turning, sew the sides and bottom together through all thicknesses. Clip the corners, turn right side out, and press. Sew the opening closed. Topstitch around the needle roll $1/2$" from the edges.

5. Pin, then sew from top to bottom every $4^{3}/_{4}$" to divide the pockets into sections.

6. Press the twill tape ends $1/4$" to the wrong side twice; hem. Sew one end to the back of the needle roll on one side. Sew half of the snap to this end of the tape. Sew the other snap half to the wrong side and the button to the right side of the other tape end. Embellish the button with a gathered ribbon scrap. Place knitting needles in the pockets and roll up to fasten.

Blanket in a Backpack

• 40" x 60" fleece rectangle for blanket • two 18" fleece squares for backpack • 3" x 14" fleece strip, cut lengthwise (not selvage to selvage) • two 28" lengths of $1^{1}/_{2}$"w webbing for straps (adjust length as needed) • two 42" lengths of 1"w webbing for drawstring

For all sewing, use a $1/2$" seam allowance unless otherwise stated.

1. For the handle, fold the long edges of the 3" x 14" strip to the center. Fold along the center and topstitch along the long edges.
2. For the drawstring casings, fold the top edge of each square 2" to the wrong side; topstitch close to the raw edge.
3. Folding one end of each strap under 2", center and pin the straps on the right side of one square just below the casing; stitch as shown in Fig. 1. Pin the opposite ends of the straps to the bottom edge of the square, 1" in from the corners. Pin the handle to the wrong side of the square.
4. With the strap side up and the casing at the top, pin the square with the straps to one upper corner of the blanket. Topstitch along the top edge of the square.
5. Matching the raw edges, pin the remaining square, wrong side up, on the square with the straps. Beginning and ending at the casing seam, sew the squares to the blanket along the side and bottom edges.
6. For the drawstrings, beginning and ending on one side of the backpack, thread one drawstring through both casings; knot the ends together. Repeat with the remaining drawstring on the opposite side of the casing. Turn the backpack right side out and tuck the blanket inside to carry.

Fig. 1

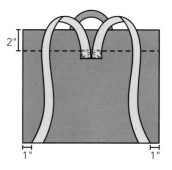

Crochet Hook Roll

- 19$\frac{1}{2}$" x 25" fabric piece for the body • 19$\frac{1}{2}$" x 12" fabric piece for the pocket • 1 yard of 1"w ribbon • $\frac{5}{8}$ yard of $\frac{3}{8}$"w ribbon • clear nylon thread
- 19$\frac{1}{2}$" x 12" piece of batting
- $\frac{5}{8}$ yard of jumbo rickrack
- two 1" rectangle rings • liquid fray preventative

For all sewing, use a $\frac{1}{2}$" seam allowance unless otherwise stated.

1. Matching the wrong sides and short ends, fold the body in half. Matching the wrong sides and long edges, fold the pocket in half. Press the folds.
2. Cut a 19$\frac{1}{2}$" length from each ribbon. Layer and pin the ribbons near the fold of the pocket; zigzag stitch with nylon thread.
3. Unfold the body wrong side up. Pin, then baste the batting to the lower half of the fabric, aligning one long edge of the batting with the fold. Leaving the piece unfolded, turn the body right side up. Aligning the raw edges, pin the pocket on the lower half of the body and pin a 19$\frac{1}{2}$" rickrack length $\frac{1}{8}$" from the bottom edge; baste along the side and bottom edges.
4. Matching right sides, refold the body. Leaving an opening on one side for turning, sew the sides and bottom together through all thicknesses. Clip the corners, turn right side out, and press. Sew the opening closed. Topstitch around the crochet hook roll $\frac{1}{4}$" from the edges.
5. Pin, then sew from top to bottom every 4$\frac{1}{2}$" to divide the pockets into sections.
6. Cut a 12" length of 1"w ribbon for the closure. Press one end $\frac{1}{4}$" to the wrong side twice; hem. Thread the hemmed end through the rings, fold, then sew across the ribbon to hold the rings in place. Sew the ribbon to the outside of the roll as shown (Fig. 1).
7. Apply fray preventative to the remaining ribbon end. Place crochet hooks in the pockets, fold the top down and roll up to fasten.

Fig. 1

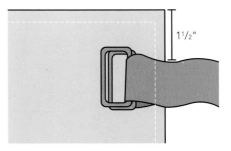

1$\frac{1}{2}$"

Patchwork Coasters

- assorted fabric for patchwork
- 5" square of backing fabric for each coaster • batting

For all sewing, match the right sides and use a 1/4" seam allowance unless otherwise stated.

1. For the coaster fronts, cut 18"-long strips of fabric, making each strip narrower at one end, but at least 1½"w (Fig. 1). Sew the strips together along the long edges, alternating the wide and narrow ends, until you roughly have an 18" square. Press all the seams in one direction.
2. Cut four 5" squares (on the diagonal) from the pieced strips. Cut four 4½" squares of batting.
3. Center and pin one batting square on the wrong side of each coaster front.
4. Leaving an opening for turning, sew the front and the backing of each coaster together. Trim the corners, turn right side out and press. Sew the openings closed.
5. Stitch "in the ditch" along the seams.

Fig. 1

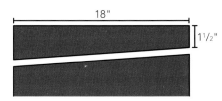

Crochet Hook Roll

Patchwork Coasters

Fig. 1 diagram labels: 18" and 1½"

Ribbon Place Mats & Napkins

Place Mats

• 20" x 14" piece of cotton or linen for each place mat base • red and green ribbons in varying widths and textures • paper-backed fusible web • pressing cloth • fabric glue • 1"w grosgrain ribbon for binding (2 yards per place mat) • liquid fray preventative

1. Fuse web to the wrong side of the base fabric. Arrange all the ribbons on the base fabric and fuse in place, using a pressing cloth and testing the iron temperature on each ribbon to prevent melting or scorching. Trim, then glue any loose ends.
2. For the binding, cut two 14" and two 20" lengths of grosgrain ribbon. Matching the long edges, press each length in half. Insert the place mat short ends into the folds of the 14" ribbon lengths; topstitch in place. Fold the ends of the 20" lengths as shown in Fig. 1, trimming the folded corners in half and applying fray preventative to the very point of the ribbon. Insert the place mat long edges into the folds of the 20" ribbon lengths; topstitch in place, carefully stitching the mitered corners.

Fig. 1

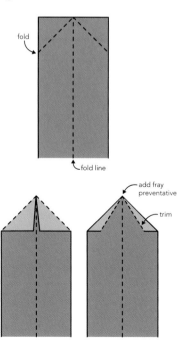

fold

fold line

add fray preventative

trim

Napkins

• napkins • fabric scraps or wide ribbon for holly leaves • paper-backed fusible web • sequins and beads

For each napkin, trace the holly pattern (page 153) onto the paper backing of the fusible web. Cut out, leaving about 1/4" around the lines. Fuse the leaf pattern to the wrong side of the fabric or ribbon. Cut out and fuse the leaf to the napkin. Add each berry by stitching through a sequin, a bead, then back through the sequin; knot on the wrong side.

Easy Apron

- 1 yard of print fabric • ½ yard of solid fabric
- 2 jingle bells

1. Matching the right sides and long edges, fold a 31"w x 33"h fabric piece in half. For the armholes, mark 9¼" from the top corner opposite the fold on the side and top edges. Use a large plate or mixing bowl to draw a curved line between the marks. Cut away the armholes and unfold the apron. Following the curve of the armhole, cut two 3" wide casing pieces from solid fabric. Press each short end 1" to the wrong side.

2. Press the straight edges of the apron piece under ⅜", then ⅝" and topstitch.

3. Match right sides and use a ¼" seam allowance to sew the casings to the apron along the short curved edges of the casings. Clip the curves to make the casings lie flat; then, press the casings to the back of the apron and press the remaining curved edges ¼" to the wrong side. Topstitch along each curved edge of the casings, leaving the ends open for the tie.

4. Cut four 1½" x 26" solid fabric strips and use a ¼" seam allowance to sew them together to make a 102½" long tie. Press each edge of the tie ¼" to the wrong side. Matching the wrong sides and long edges, press the tie in half. Topstitch along each edge of the tie. Thread each end through an armhole casing and sew jingle bells to the ends.

✻ *23*

Winking Santa

• craft knife • 3" dia. foam ball and $4^7/_8$"h foam egg for the head and body • craft glue • scrap foam • scrap poster board • $4^1/_2$" dia. foam ring • Creative Paperclay® • palette knife • sandpaper • acrylic paints and paintbrushes • disposable foam brush • glitter and mica flakes • 12" square of red fabric for hat • faux fur

1. For Santa's framework, cut a small notch in the head so it will rest on the tip of the body and glue them together (see photo, page 27). Glue leg/feet shapes cut from scrap foam to the body. Glue a poster board oval to the feet for a base. For the arms, cut arcs (about $4^1/_2$" long, measured along the outer edge) from the ring and glue to the body.
2. Cover the framework with Paperclay, dipping your finger in water and smoothing the clay as you go. Build the clay up for the facial details, hair, beard, mittens, boots, and snow-covered base. Use the palette knife to add texture to the beard and hair. As the clay dries, it may crack; fill in with more Paperclay. Allow to dry overnight. Lightly sand, then paint Santa.
3. Brush glue on the boots and base. Sprinkle the boots with glitter and the base with mica flakes.
4. Enlarge the hat pattern (page 157) to 151%. Matching the pattern fold line to the fold of the fabric, cut out the hat. Matching the right sides and raw edges, use a $1/_4$" seam allowance to sew the hat along the straight edge. Turn right side out.
5. Glue the hat to Santa's head. Glue strips of fur to the hat, coat, and boot tops.

Christmas Kids

• craft knife • foam ball for each head (we used 1" and $1^1/_2$" dia. balls) • foam egg for each body (we used $2^1/_2$" and 3"h eggs) • craft glue • scrap foam • scrap poster board • Creative Paperclay® • sandpaper • acrylic paints and paintbrushes • fine-point permanent marker • disposable foam brush • mica flakes

1. For each child figure, cut a small notch in the head so it will rest on the tip of the body and glue them together (see photo, page 27). Glue leg shapes cut from scrap foam to the body. Glue a poster board round or oval to the feet for a base.
2. Cover the framework with Paperclay, dipping your finger in water and smoothing the clay as you go. Build the clay up for the facial features, clothing details, snow-covered base, and to smooth feet and legs. Make separate arm pieces and add while they are wet. Allow to dry overnight. Lightly sand, then paint the figure. Add details with the marker.
3. Brush glue on the base; sprinkle with mica flakes.

Cone Trees

• foam cones (various sizes) • Creative Paperclay® • fine-grit sandpaper • acrylic paints and paintbrushes • clear acrylic spray sealer • craft glue • assorted buttons

Cover the cones with Paperclay, building up the clay at the top to create a nice rounded point on the tree. Make the clay as smooth as possible, dipping your finger in water and smoothing the clay as you go. As the clay dries, it may crack; fill in any cracks with more Paperclay. Once completely dry, sand the trees until they are smooth. Paint the trees, using several coats of paint. Spray with acrylic sealer in a well-ventilated area. Glue buttons to the trees.

Glitzen Reindeer

• craft knife • 3" dia. foam ball and 4⅞"h foam egg for the head and body • craft glue • handsaw • ⅜" dia. dowel • drill and bit • 4" dia. x 1" thick foam base • Creative Paperclay® • ⅛" dia. armature wire • floral tape • sandpaper • acrylic paints and paintbrushes • black permanent marker • printed felt • medium-gauge wire • wire cutters • needle-nose pliers • disposable foam brush • glitter • cardboard letter cutouts (ours spell "Jingle") • sharp needle • jump rings • tiny jingle bells • ribbon • metallic cord • brads

1. Cut a small notch in the head so it will rest on the tip of the body and glue them together (see photo, below). Cut 3"-long arms and 6"-long legs from the dowel. Drill a small hole through both ends of the dowel arms. Cut holes in the base for the legs and glue them in place. Insert the legs in the bottom of the body.
2. Cover the framework with Paperclay, dipping your finger in water and smoothing the clay as you go. Build the clay up in the muzzle and knee areas. Make separate ear pieces and add them while they are wet. Shape antlers from armature wire wrapped with floral tape and insert them into the head. Allow to dry overnight. Lightly sand, then paint the figure and each arm. Add a seasonal message to the base.

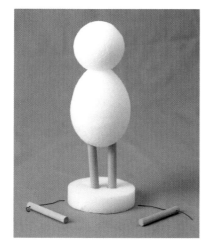

3. Make a vest from felt and wrap it around the body. Attach each arm to the body with a 4" wire length, poking the wire through the vest and into the body; coil the wire ends to secure. Brush glue and sprinkle glitter as desired. Brush the letter cutouts with glue; sprinkle with glitter.
4. For the banner, poke a hole through the top of each letter and attach a jump ring. Thread the rings and bells onto a wire length. Tie short ribbon pieces along the wire. Thread the wire ends through the hoof holes and secure. Fashion a bridle and reins from metallic cord and brads, gluing the cord ends behind the brads.

Tags, Cards, & Wraps

Settle in for a pleasant evening of fashioning greeting cards, gift tags, bags, and wraps that will get lots of "oohs" and "aahs."

Nativity Silhouette Card

- tracing paper • cardstock
- removable double-sided tape
- craft knife and cutting mat
- craft glue • disposable foam brush • very fine glitter
- adhesive foam dots • ribbon

Trace the pattern (page 149). Adhere the pattern to cardstock with removable tape. Cut out the silhouette with the craft knife. Spread glue over the silhouette and sprinkle with glitter. For the card, match the short edges and fold a 6" x 8" cardstock piece in half. Adhere the glittered piece to the front of the card with foam dots. Tie a bow around the card front.

Embroidered Card

- tracing paper • fusible stabilizer • silk fabric scrap
- water-soluble marking pen
- embroidery floss • spray adhesive • cardstock • craft knife and cutting mat • craft glue • sequins • small beads

Trace the pattern (page 149). Fuse stabilizer to the wrong side of the silk fabric. Trace "Merry Christmas" onto the silk with the marking pen. Work Stem Stitch (page 141) words with 3 strands of embroidery floss. Working in a well-ventilated area, use spray adhesive to adhere the embroidered fabric to a 7$1/8$" x 4$1/4$" cardstock piece, centering the words. Trim the excess fabric. For the card, match the short edges and fold a 7$3/4$" x 10" cardstock piece in half. Cut a 6$3/8$" x 3$1/2$" window in the card front. Machine stitch the embroidered piece to the back of the window. Embellish the corners with sequins and beads.

Painted Postcard
(shown on page 30)

- transfer paper • 5" x 7" canvas board • acrylic paints and paintbrushes (refer to pattern, page 148) • clear matte acrylic sealer • craft glue • cardstock

Enlarge the pattern (page 148) to 134%. Transfer the pattern (page 142) to the canvas board. (We've given you the whole flower—position it however you like.) Lightly erase the transferred lines so you can barely see them. Paint the design. After the paint dries, apply several coats of sealer for safe traveling. Glue cardstock on the back. Address the card, write a message, and add postage.

Embroidered Card
Nativity Silhouette Card

Painted Postcard
Instructions on page 28.

Framed Family Tree

- picture frame (we used an 11" x 14" frame)
- decorative paper • craft glue • assorted cardstock • photocopied family photos
- decorative-edged scissors • adhesive foam dots • ribbons • ornament cardstock die-cuts
- star punches • rub-on letters • brad

1. Discard the glass and remove the backing from the picture frame; cover the backing with decorative paper.
2. Center the frame over the backing. Arrange, then trim your photos to stack into a tree shape within the frame opening. Adhere each photo to layered cardstock; trim with decorative-edged scissors. Glue the photos to the backing, inserting a ribbon loop "trunk" under the bottom center photo. Punch stars from cardstock; use foam dots to layer atop the photos. Add ribbon-embellished die-cut ornaments with foam dots.
3. For the nameplate, cut and layer cardstock pieces. Add the family name with rub-on letters. Attach the ribbon trim with a brad. Secure the nameplate to the frame with foam dots.

Santa Gift Bag

- gift bag • 1/4" dia. hole punch • wire-edged ribbon • Santa faces stamp • black ink pad • white and red cardstock • colored pencils
- mini pom-poms • craft glue • button • 3 mini jingle bells
- mulberry paper • vellum • checked trim • adhesive foam dots

1. Punch holes, 2" apart, at the top center of the bag, punching through all the layers. Thread ribbon through the holes and tie in a bow.
2. Stamp and color the Santa faces on white cardstock. Machine stitch a border around the image. Trim the cardstock about 1/8" from the stitching. Glue the pom-poms and button to the cardstock. Use thread to tie each bell to the button.
3. Use foam dots to attach the Santa cardstock to a layered cardstock, mulberry paper, and vellum card with checked trim. Layer the card on another cardstock piece; glue to the bag front.

"Merry Christmas" Bag

- 17" x 16 1/4" piece each of 100% rayon velvet and fabric for lining • "Merry Christmas" stamp • white paint pen • white chenille rickrack

For all sewing, match the right sides and use a 1/4" seam allowance unless otherwise stated.

1. To emboss the velvet, place the "Merry Christmas" stamp right side up on a flat surface. With the long edge at the top, center the right side of the velvet on the right side of the stamp. Lightly spray the wrong side of the velvet with water. Place a warm iron on the wrong side of the velvet for 15 to 20 seconds. Use the paint pen to color the embossed letters.
2. Sew the short ends of the velvet piece together. With the seam at the center back, sew across the bottom of the bag; turn the bag right side out. Repeat to sew the lining, leaving an opening for turning in the bottom seam; do not turn the lining right side out.
3. Matching right sides, place the bag in the lining. With the rickrack sandwiched between the lining and the bag, sew the lining to the bag. Turn the bag right side out. Sew the opening closed. Fold the top of the bag down 3" to show off the lining.

Santa Gift Bag

"Merry Christmas" Bag

"Merry Christmas" Card

"Merry Christmas" Card
- "Merry Christmas" stamp
- red and white cardstock • red ink pad • print vellum • craft knife and cutting mat • craft glue • vellum tape • border stickers • 4 buttons

1. Stamp "Merry Christmas" in the center of a 5$\frac{1}{2}$" x 7$\frac{1}{2}$" white cardstock piece.
2. For the card, match the short ends of an 8" x 12" red cardstock piece and fold in half. Cut a piece of print vellum slightly smaller than the card. Centering the stamped image under the vellum, draw a window over the image; cut out the vellum window.
3. Layer and attach the stamped image and vellum on the card. Adhere border stickers along the edges of the vellum. Add buttons to the window corners.

Recipe File with Recipe Cards
- expandable check file • photocopied family photos • spray adhesive • assorted cardstock die-cuts • alphabet stickers • buttons • hot glue gun • cardstock • double-sided tape

Always work in a well-ventilated area when using spray adhesive.

1. Trim a photo to fit on the expandable file. Adhere the photo and die-cuts to the file. Personalize with alphabet stickers. Hot glue buttons to the file.
2. Using your computer, print recipe category titles. Cut a cardstock tab for each category. Adhere the printed titles to the tabs. Tape the tabs to the file dividers.
3. For each recipe card, adhere the recipe (printed from your computer), a mini photo, and die-cuts on a cardstock rectangle.

Santa Card

- assorted cardstock • Santa and holiday sentiment stamps • black ink pad • colored pencils • craft glue • ribbon • brad • adhesive foam dots • oval and circle paper punches (optional) • embroidery floss • button

1. For the card, match the short edges of a 10" x 7" cardstock piece and fold in half.
2. Stamp Santa on white cardstock. Color the design. Trim, then lightly ink the cardstock edges.
3. Cut 2 layers of cardstock slightly larger than the Santa-stamped piece. Glue the bottom layer to the card. Wrapping the ends to the wrong side, glue a ribbon around the card. Embellish the ribbon with a brad. Adhere the remaining layer and Santa image to the card with foam dots.
4. Stamp the sentiment on white cardstock; cut or punch out in an oval shape. Use foam dots to adhere the sentiment to a larger cardstock oval. Punch or cut a cardstock circle. Tie a floss bow through the button. Glue the oval, circle, and button to the card.

Santa Card

Snowflake Tag

Ornaments Tag

Snowflake Tag

- assorted cardstock • snowflakes stamp
- black pigment ink pad • silver embossing powder • heat embossing tool • craft glue
- 1/8" dia. hole punch • brad • ribbon

1. Stamp the snowflakes on cardstock. While the ink is still wet, sprinkle with embossing powder; shake off the excess. Use the embossing tool to heat the embossing powder.
2. Trim the snowflake-stamped cardstock to a tag shape. Cut 3 more layers of cardstock tags, each slightly larger than the last. Lightly ink the edges. Glue the 2 bottom tags together. Glue the top 2 tags together.
3. Holding all tags together, punch a hole near the top and attach a brad. Attach a ribbon loop to the tag back.

Ornaments Tag

- assorted cardstock • ornaments stamp
- black ink pad • colored pencils • embroidery floss • craft glue • ribbon • decorative and plain brads • charm • adhesive foam dots

1. Stamp and color the ornaments on cardstock. Add floss ornament hangers and bows. Trim the ornament-stamped cardstock to a tag shape.
2. Cut 3 more layers of cardstock tags, each slightly larger than the last. Lightly ink the edges. Glue the 2 bottom tags together. Cut a slit near the top and knot a ribbon hanger on the tag.
3. Glue the top 2 tags together. Add a decorative brad to the tag top. Attach a charm to the tag with a plain brad.
4. Use foam dots to attach the top tags to the bottom tags.

Happy Gift Tag

- white cardstock • glass jar
- velvet ribbon • brad

To make this cute candy jar, color copy the tag (page 143) onto cardstock and cut it out. Wrap ribbon around the jar and attach the tag to the ribbon with the brad.

Package Tags

Create a keepsake monogram by placing a sticker on an acrylic oval and spraying with a frosted glass spray. A scalloped paper background adhered to the wrong side of the oval completes the look.

A small photo frame looks lovely with a seasonal sticker and coordinating paper.

Dress up an elegant ornament even more by accenting the design with adhesive-backed rhinestones and adding the recipient's name to a sparkly mini frame.

Ready-made tags get a special touch when decorated with festive rub-on sentiments.

Reusable Wrapped Box

- papier-mâché box • ribbon to cover box lid • double-sided tape
- fabric to cover box • water-soluble fabric marker • fabric glue
- disposable foam brush • ribbon to tie box • floral wire • small ornaments

1. To cover the box lid, tape ribbons to the lid, wrapping the ribbon ends to the inside. Add as many or as few as you wish. Wrap a ribbon around the lid sides.
2. Referring to Fig. 1, measure the box along A, B, and C. Using the formulas below, cut a fabric piece the determined measurements.
   Fabric Width = (A x 2) + B + 3"
   Fabric Length = (A x 2) + C + 3"
3. Center the box on the wrong side of the fabric. Draw around the box bottom and extend the sides with a ruler and fabric marker. Referring to Fig. 2, cut the corners from the fabric 1/2" outside the drawn lines; snip 1/2" into the corners. Press flaps on opposite ends 1/2" to the wrong side.
4. Brush glue on the box bottom. Center the box bottom on the wrong side of the fabric. Brush glue on the box sides and approximately 1 1/2" down into the box. Glue the unpressed fabric flaps to the sides of the box, wrapping the fabric edges around the corners; fold the excess into the box (Fig. 3). Repeat with the pressed flaps, covering the raw side edges of the fabric (Fig. 4). Glue ribbon over the raw fabric edges inside the box.
5. Tie a ribbon around the box. Wire the ornaments to the ribbon bow.

Reusable Wrapped Box

Fig. 1

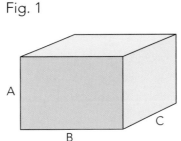

Fig. 2

Fig. 3

Fig. 4

Fabric Mini Gift Bags

- 8½" x 7¼" fabric piece for bag • rub-on letter • clothespin • tracing paper • water-soluble fabric marker • two 5" fabric squares for flower • scalloped pinking shears • felt scrap • button • fabric glue

For all sewing, match the right sides and use a ¼" seam allowance unless otherwise stated.

1. For each bag, press one long edge of the fabric rectangle ¼" to the wrong side twice; hem. Matching short edges, fold the rectangle in half. Sew along the side and bottom edges; turn right side out.
2. Apply the rub-on to the clothespin.
3. Trace the petal pattern (page 149) onto tracing paper and cut out. Use the fabric marker to draw around the pattern, making 5 petals on one fabric square, leaving ½" between petals.
4. Matching the wrong sides, pin the squares together and sew along the drawn lines. Use pinking shears to cut out the petals ⅛" larger than the stitching lines. Cut two 1" dia. felt circles. Pleat the petal points and glue them between the felt circles. Sew the button to the flower. Glue the flower to the clothespin.

Fabric Mini Gift Bags

Prettily Wrapped Packages

Prettily Wrapped Packages

It doesn't take much more paper or time to create a lovely package with four smooth sides.

To cover a box, cut wrapping paper wide enough to overlap in the middle and long enough for the folded ends to fold underneath the box (Fig. 1).

Tape the overlapping ends to the bottom of the box (Fig. 2). *(The dashed lines indicate the box outline.)*

From each end, cut paper as shown (Fig. 3).

Tucking in the sides, crease and fold each end over the box bottom (Figs. 4-7), taping as necessary. This creates four smooth sides on the package.

Fig. 1

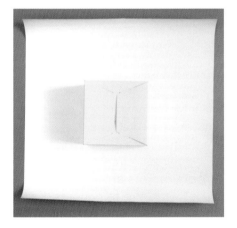

Fig. 2

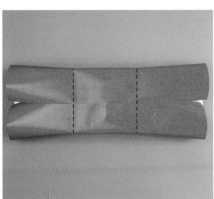

Fig. 3

Fig. 4

Fig. 5

Fig. 6

Fig. 7

Christmas Keepsakes hold memories
so dear, they will be the last items put away after the season ends.
Advent and tree section ornaments, decorations made from
vintage jewelry—each will be treasured for years to come.

Advent Countdown Ornaments

Counting down the days till Christmas is even more fun when you add a new ornament to the tree each day.

• large lidded box that will hold 24 glass ball ornaments (our box is 19" x 12" x 3") • wrapping paper • $3/8$"w ribbon • craft glue • double-sided adhesive sheets • matte finish glass ball ornaments • bone folder • fine glitter • 1"w ribbon • silver cupcake baking cups • glue pen (optional)

1. Glue the wrapping paper to the inside bottom of the box. Glue the narrow ribbon along the inside edge of the box.
2. Using your computer, print out numbers 1-24, in a pretty font and a point size appropriate for the ball ornaments. Trace the numbers onto the adhesive sheets, using a light box or a sunny window; cut out.
3. Adhere the numbers to the ball ornaments. Carefully burnish the edges with the bone folder. Peel off the remaining adhesive backing. If some of the adhesive comes off with the backing, use the glue pen to fill in the number.
4. Sprinkle the adhesive with glitter; allow to dry. Tie a wide ribbon bow to each ornament. Place the baking cups in the box and place an ornament in each.

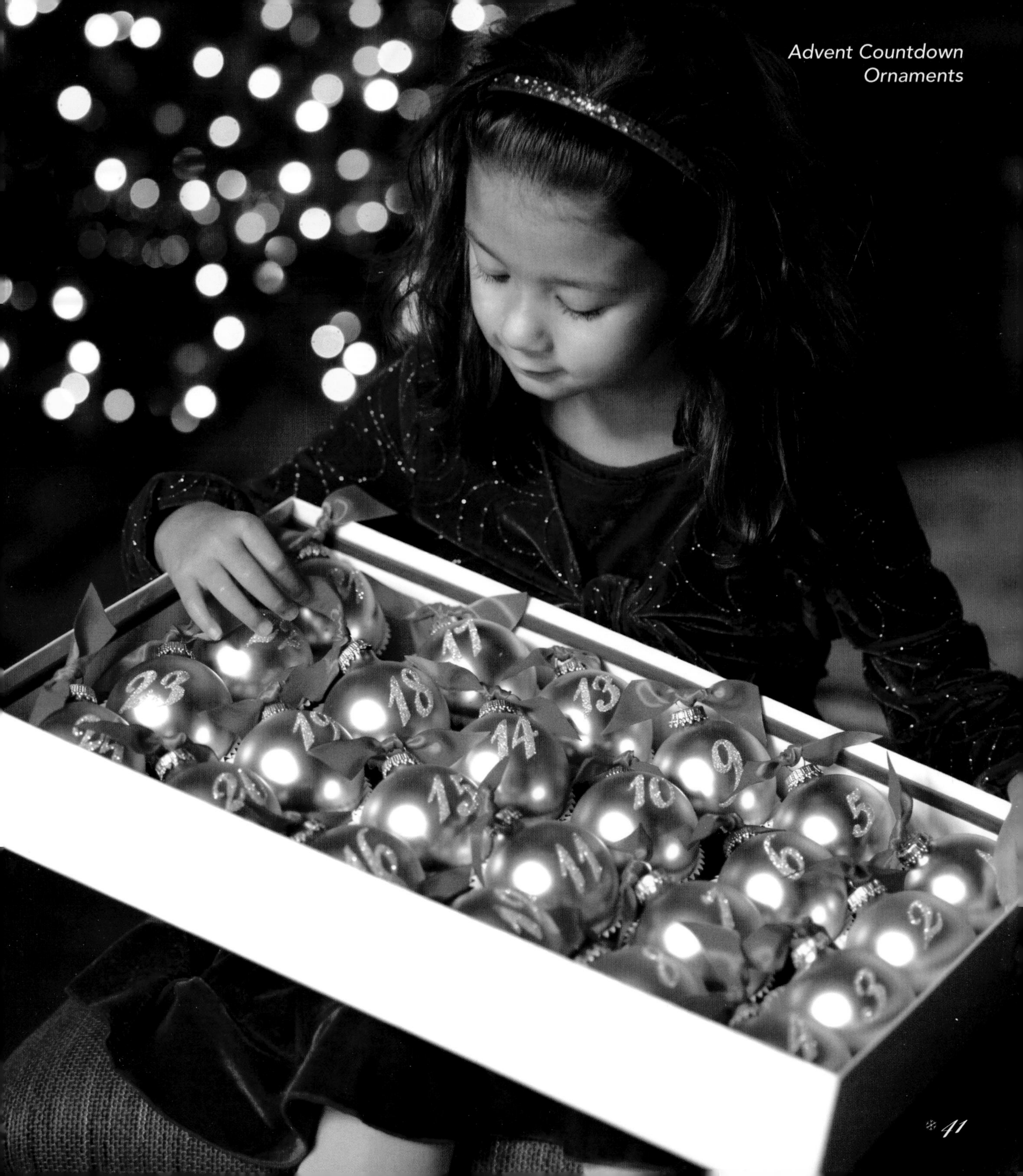

Advent Countdown Ornaments

Framed Heirloom Jewelry

• 8" x 10" photo frame • velvet for background cardboard
• hot glue gun • 7½" cardboard square • velvet to cover
cardboard • assorted pieces of jewelry (vintage, new, family
pieces), buttons, beads, and charms • large jewelry piece accent

1. Discard the glass from the frame. Glue the background velvet
   to the frame back.
2. For the wreath, cut a 6½" diameter cardboard ring with a 4"
   diameter center opening. Glue a piece of velvet to the ring,
   wrapping the excess to the wrong side, clipping curves, and
   trimming as necessary. Glue the ring to the center of the frame
   back. Replace the frame back and any other backing materials
   in the frame.
3. Arrange all jewelry, buttons, beads, and charms on the fabric-
   covered ring, layering the pieces as desired and placing the
   large accent piece on the uppermost layer. Once you are
   happy with the arrangement, glue each piece in place.

Heirloom Jewelry Ornaments

• poster board • gold spray
paint • foam core board • velvet
to cover foam core on both
sides • hot glue gun • clear
nylon thread • pinking shears
• assorted pieces of jewelry
(vintage, new, family pieces),
buttons, beads, and charms
• string pearls or beads

1. For each ornament, enlarge a
   pattern (page 148) to 136%.
   Use the patterns and cut the
   shape from poster board.
   Spray paint the shape in a
   well-ventilated area.
2. Cut a foam core board shape
   somewhat larger than the
   poster board shape (we
   cut rectangle, circle, and
   diamond shapes). Glue velvet
   to one side of the foam core,
   wrapping the excess to the
   wrong side and trimming
   as necessary. Glue a nylon
   thread hanger to the back.
   Use the pinking shears to
   cut a piece of velvet slightly
   smaller than the foam core.
   Glue to the back of the foam
   core.
3. Glue the painted shape to
   the velvet-covered foam
   core. Arrange all jewelry,
   buttons, beads, and charms,
   layering the pieces as
   desired; then, glue each
   piece in place. Glue string
   pearls along the edges.

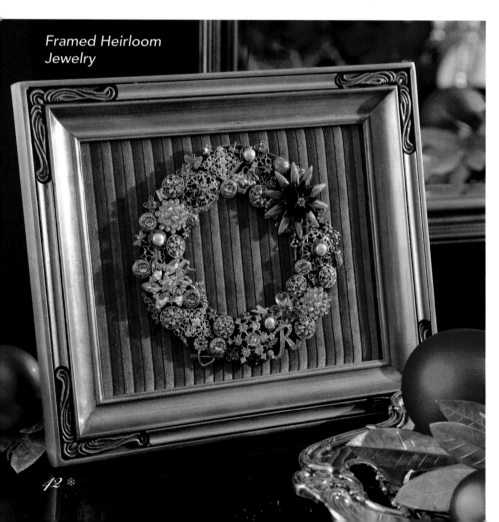

Framed Heirloom Jewelry

Heirloom Jewelry Ornaments

Tree Trunk Ornaments

Tree Trunk Ornaments

• ¼" slice of tree trunk (from last year's tree)
• paint pens, markers, rub-ons, rubber stamps, glitter, ink, or acrylic paints to decorate ornaments • clear acrylic spray sealer • drill with ⅛" bit • ribbon, cord, or swirl ornament hanger and jump ring

Create a new keepsake each year with a dried sliver cut from last year's tree. Here are a few ideas to get you started.

For a contemporary look, dot a border around a painted circle with a fine-point permanent pen and freehand a verse—"o Christmas tree" is a natural. Record the year with a metallic paint pen.

Scallop the edges of baby's first Christmas photo. Preserve the year with rub-ons on a ribbon banner, glued across the bottom.

For elegant simplicity, rub on a Christmas greeting and add luster with clear glaze.

Not artistic? Use stamps, ink, and glitter to create the design.

Working in a well-ventilated area, spray each ornament with 2 coats of sealer. To hang the ornament, drill a small hole through the top and attach a swirl hanger with a large jump ring (page 142) or tie a ribbon or cord loop.

Village Play Mat

- 36" x 38" piece each of background and backing fabric • ½ yard of black fabric • scrap fabrics for appliqués (blue, brown, dark green, light green, purple, red, white, and yellow) • paper-backed fusible web • white acrylic paint and a small round paintbrush • 2⅓ yards of 1"w nylon webbing for handles

For all sewing, match the right sides and use a ½" seam allowance unless otherwise stated.

1. Enlarge the patterns (pages 150-151) to 121%. Trace the patterns on the paper side of the web, tracing the number of pieces indicated on the patterns and leaving about ½" between the pieces. Cut out slightly outside the drawn lines.
2. Fuse the web pieces to the wrong side of the appliqué fabrics; cut along the drawn lines. Arrange and fuse the appliqués on the background fabric (Diagram, page 150).
3. Paint the lane dividing line on the road.
4. Cut web 1" smaller than the backing fabric, piecing as necessary. Center and fuse on the wrong side of the backing fabric. Do *not* remove the paper backing.
5. For the handle, sew the ends of the nylon webbing together; finger press the seam allowances open. Place the webbing on the right side of the backing fabric. Sew the webbing to the backing where shown by the dashed lines (Fig. 1).
6. Sew the mat and backing together, leaving an opening for turning. Remove the paper backing. Clip the corners, turn right side out, and sew the opening closed.
7. Fuse the mat and backing together. To fold for carrying, fold the mat lengthwise into thirds, then fold the ends toward the center.

Fig. 1

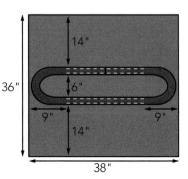

Tassels Hat (grey)
Pom-Pom Hat (blue)
Rosebud Hat (pink)

Child's Knit Hat, Three Ways

- Bulky Weight Yarn ⑤ BULKY
  [3½ ounces, 121 yards
  (100 grams, 110 meters)
  per skein **or** 3 ounces,
  135 yards (85 grams,
  123 meters) per skein] -
  1 skein
- Straight knitting needles, size
  10 (6 mm) **or** size needed for
  gauge • Yarn needle

Finished Size:
Small{Medium-Large}
Head Circumference:
14½{17-19½}"/37{43-49.5} cm

Size Note: Instructions are
written for size Small with sizes
Medium and Large in braces
{ }. Instructions will be easier
to read if you circle all the
numbers pertaining to your size.
If only one number is given, it
applies to all sizes.

GAUGE: In Stockinette Stitch,
15 sts = 4" (10 cm)

HAT
Cast on 57{65-73} sts.
Row 1 (Right side): Knit across.

Row 2: Purl across.
Row 3: K1, (P2, K6) across.
Row 4: (P6, K2) across to last st, P1.
Row 5: Knit across.
Row 6: Purl across.
Row 7: K5, P2, (K6, P2) across to
last 2 sts, K2.
Row 8: P2, K2, (P6, K2) across to
last 5 sts, P5.
For Pom-Pom or Tassels
finishing, repeat Rows 1-8 until
piece measures approximately
7{8-9}"/18{20.5-23} cm from cast
on edge, ending by working a
wrong side row.
Bind off all sts in **knit.**

For Rosebud finishing, repeat Rows 1-8 until piece measures approximately 8{9-10}"/20.5{23-25.5} cm from cast on edge, ending by working a **wrong** side row.
Bind off all sts in **knit**.

FINISHING
With **wrong** side together, weave the short edges together to form a ring (**Fig. 1, page 140**).

For Pom-Pom:
With seam at back, sew top edge; then bring points together at center top of Hat and tack in place. Make a 1¹/₂" dia. Pom-Pom (**Figs. 3a-c, page 141**). Attach Pom-Pom to top of Hat.

For Rosebud:
Thread a yarn needle with an 18" (45.5 cm) length of yarn. Weave needle through sts 1" (2.5 cm) down from top, gather tightly, and secure end.
Rosebud (Make 2)
Cast on 14 sts **leaving a long end for sewing**. Beginning with a **purl** row, work in Stockinette Stitch for 5 rows. Bind off all sts in **knit**. Using photo as a guide, roll piece into a Rosebud. Thread needle with long end and sew base of Rosebud; do **not** cut yarn. Using photo as a guide, sew each Rosebud to Hat.

For Tassels:
With seam at back, sew top edge. Make two 2¹/₂" (6.5 cm) Tassels (**Figs. 2a & b, page 140**). Attach one Tassel to each corner of Hat.

Cozy Cottage
• papier-mâché house • craft glue • cardboard • acrylic paint and paintbrushes • ribbon or scrapbook paper scraps • Snow-tex™ textural medium • palette knife • coarse glitter • mini bottle brush trees

Glue the house to a cardboard base. Paint the house and trim. Glue ribbon or scrapbook paper scraps to the window for shutters. Apply textural medium to the roof, chimney, and base; sprinkle glitter into the "snow" while still wet. Shake off the excess. Glue the trees to the base.

"Gingerbread" House

• lightweight corrugated cardboard • 5¼" x 8¾" x 7" box (we used a 92 ounce laundry detergent box) • hot glue gun • white acrylic paint • paintbrush • items to decorate the house (we used mini vanilla wafers, sugar wafers, butter cookies, hard candies, candy canes, gumdrops, chewy candy shapes, candy-coated fruit chews, red licorice whips, and bell-shaped candy) • white dimensional paint • spray snow

1. Referring to the Diagram (right), cut the front/back pieces from cardboard. Cut two 7" x 9" side pieces and two 4" x 9" roof pieces. Cut one 8" x 10" base piece.
2. Center and glue the box on the base. Glue the front, back, and sides to the box. Glue the roof pieces to the sides; glue the top edges together.
3. Paint the roof and door.
4. Glue cookies and candies to the house.
5. Outline the windows, cookies, and candies and fill in any gaps with the dimensional paint. Working in a well-ventilated area, lightly spray snow on the house.

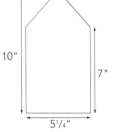

10"

7"

5¼"

Crazy Quilt Stocking

• 12" x 20" muslin piece • fabric scraps • 12" x 20" stocking back fabric piece • two 12" x 20" lining fabric pieces • 2" x 16¼" binding fabric strip • ribbon for hanger

1. To make the crazy quilt fabric, cut 1 fabric scrap with straight edges. Place this piece, right side up, in the center of the muslin piece. Cut another scrap with one edge the same length as one edge of first scrap.
2. Trim the second scrap so that once it is sewn down, the pieced area will not have any inside angles. With the right sides facing, lay the second scrap on the first scrap. Using a ¼" seam allowance and sewing through all 3 layers, sew the scraps together along the matched edge. Press the second scrap right side up.
3. Cut a third scrap with one edge the same length as one edge of the pieced area. Repeat Step 2 with the third scrap.
4. Repeat Step 3, adding scraps until the entire muslin piece is covered.
5. Enlarge the stocking pattern (page 152) to 213%.
6. Follow Steps 2-3, using the muslin piece as the stocking front, and Steps 5-7 of Cuffed Stocking (facing page) to complete the stocking.

"Gingerbread" House

Cuffed Stocking

For all sewing, match the right sides of the fabric unless otherwise stated.

• two 12" x 20" stocking fabric pieces • two 12" x 20" lining fabric pieces • 7" x 19" felt piece for cuff • 2" x 16¼" binding fabric strip • ribbon for hanger • 6 jingle bells • hot glue gun

1. Enlarge the patterns (page 152) to 213%. Using the cuff pattern, cut 1 felt cuff; set aside.
2. Cut out the stocking pattern. Draw around the pattern on the wrong side of one stocking fabric piece. Leaving the top edge open, sew the stocking pieces together, stitching on the drawn line. Cut out the stocking about ½" outside the stitching line. Clip the curves, turn right side out, and press.
3. Repeat Step 2 with the lining fabric pieces; do not turn the lining right side out. Matching the wrong sides, insert the lining into the stocking.
4. Match the ends and fold the cuff piece in half. Use a ⅜" seam allowance to sew the ends together; press the seam allowances open and turn the cuff right side out. With the wrong side of the cuff facing the right side of the stocking and matching

Crazy Quilt Stocking
Cuffed Stocking

the cuff seam to the heel-side seam, baste the cuff to the stocking along the top edge.
5. Press one end of the binding fabric strip ½" to the wrong side. Match the wrong sides and press the strip in half lengthwise; unfold. Press the long edges to the center; refold the binding.
6. Sandwich the binding over the top edge of the stocking, overlapping the unpressed edge with the pressed edge. Topstitch the binding to the stocking.
7. Tack the ends of a ribbon loop inside the stocking at the heel-side seam.
8. Glue the bells to the cuff points.

Christmas Card Globes

Polka Dot Pot

Bird Ornament

Christmas Card Globes

• clear acrylic separating ball ornaments • craft glue
• disposable foam brush
• glitter • Christmas cards
• cardstock • embroidery floss
• ribbon • jingle bell • tag

For the large ornament, separate the ornament pieces. Spread glue inside one half and sprinkle glitter in the ornament. When dry, shake off the excess. Cut an image from a Christmas card about $1/2$" smaller than the ornament. Cut a piece of cardstock the same size. Sandwiching a length of floss in between, glue the circles together. Apply glitter to the outer edges. Thread floss through the opening at the top of the ornament and pull taut to bring the image close to the top; knot tightly. Close the ornament and tie a ribbon hanger and bow at the top. Tie a jingle bell and tag to the floss. For the small ornament, don't glitter the inside. Instead, spread glue and glitter on the ornament top before adding the ribbon hanger.

Beaded Pens

• ink pen • heavy-duty double-sided tape • seed and bugle beads • tiny glass marbles

Cover most of the pen with the tape; then, press the beads onto the tape. Fill in any spaces with marbles.

Bird Ornament

• tracing paper • double-sided patterned cardstock • gold cardstock for beak • felt • craft glue • wiggle eyes • small hole punch • small sharp scissors • ribbon

Trace the patterns (page 153). Using the patterns, cut a bird from double-sided cardstock, a gold cardstock beak, and one felt wing set. Glue the folded beak and the eyes to the bird. Punch and cut the holes in the bird as shown on the pattern; finger-pleat the wings and insert through the center hole. Thread ribbon through the remaining hole and knot the ends.

Polka Dot Pot

• flowerpot • red and white acrylic paints and paintbrush
• round sponge dauber
• coarse glitter • wrapped peppermints

Paint the flowerpot red, inside and out. Paint the outer rim white. Use the sponge dauber to stamp circles on the pot. While the paint is still wet, sprinkle the white areas with glitter. Shake off the excess. Fill the pot with peppermints.

Beaded Pens

Beribboned Stockings
- felt • fabric glue • ribbon and rickrack scraps

Enlarge the stocking pattern (page 152) to 140%. For each stocking, use the pattern and cut 2 stockings from felt. Using a $1/4$" seam allowance and leaving the top edge open, sew the stocking pieces together. Glue ribbon and rickrack to the stocking front; trim any excess.

Clothespin Kids

- wooden doll pins • 1" wooden doll pin stands • 1¼" dia. wooden beads for heads • acrylic paints and paintbrush • craft glue • chenille stem • ⁵⁄₁₆" dia. red wooden beads for hands • craft thread • tracing paper • felt • pinking shears • ³⁄₈" dia. pom-poms • ribbon

For each kid, paint the doll pin, stand, and large bead. Glue the doll pin into the bead and the stand. For the arms, bend and glue a 3½" chenille stem length just below the back of the head. Glue the red beads to the chenille stem ends. Glue craft thread lengths to the head for hair. Paint the facial features. Trace the patterns (page 153). Using the patterns, cut the hat (and skirt, if making the girl) from felt. Glue the hat together along the straight edges. Glue the hat on the head; glue a pom-pom to the hat. Wrap and glue a ribbon length around the doll's "waist." For the girl, wrap and glue the skirt just below the ribbon.

Holly Gift Bag

- 4½" x 12" felt piece for bag • felt for leaves • embroidery floss • ⁵⁄₈" dia. felt ball • craft glue • ribbon

Enlarge the holly pattern (page 153) to 213%. Cut 2 holly leaves from felt. Attach the leaves to the upper half of the bag by working Running Stitches (page 141) with 6 strands of floss. Cut the felt ball in half and glue below the leaves. Fold the bag in half and work Running Stitches on each side. Tack the ribbon ends to the sides of the bag.

Clothespin Kids

Holly Gift Bag

Snowman Candle Holder

• round votive candle holder (we used a frosted-glass holder) • black and orange dimensional paint • ribbon • craft glue • votive candle

Paint the snowman's face on the candle holder. Knot the center of a 6" ribbon length. Clip the ribbon ends to "fringe" the scarf. Glue the scarf to the candle holder and add the candle.

Never leave burning candles unattended.

Knit Scarf

finished size: 4" x 60" (10 cm x 152.5 cm)
• scraps of bulky weight yarn • straight knitting needles, size 5 (10mm) • crochet hook for fringe

Scarf

Note: *Change colors as desired. To add more texture, alternate using 1 or 2 strands of yarn.*

With the first color, cast on 10 sts.
Work in Stockinette Stitch (knit 1 row, purl 1 row) until Scarf measures about 60" (152.5 cm) from the cast on edge, ending by working a **purl** row. Bind off all sts in **knit**.

Fringe

Cut a piece of cardboard 3" (7.5 cm) wide and 9" (23 cm) long. Wind the yarn **loosely** and **evenly** lengthwise around the cardboard until the card is filled, then cut across one end; repeat as needed.
Holding 2 strands of yarn together, fold in half. With the **wrong** side facing and using a crochet hook, draw the folded end up through a stitch and pull the loose ends through the folded end; draw the knot up **tightly**. Repeat, spacing as desired across the short edges of the Scarf.
Lay the Scarf flat on a hard surface and trim the ends.

Knit Scarf

Santa Stepping Stone

• 12" dia. concrete garden stepping stone • transfer paper • acrylic paints and paintbrushes • medium point felt-tip marker • clear acrylic spray sealer

Enlarge the patterns (page 155) to 161%. Transfer the pattern onto the garden stone. Paint the design. Use the marker to add details. Working in a well-ventilated area, spray with 3-4 coats of sealer.

Santa Stepping Stone

Home Sweet Home
Mug & Mat

Etched Nativity Shade

Home Sweet Home Mug & Mat

- ceramic mug • enamel glass paint and paintbrush • tracing paper • felt • embroidery floss
- 1-2 teaspoons whole cloves
- ½ cup rice

1. Paint the design on the mug.
2. Trace the patterns (page 155). Using the patterns, cut felt flowers and flower centers. Cut two 5½" felt squares.
3. Use 6 strands of floss to work Cross Stitches (page 141), attaching each flower and flower center to one felt square.
4. Leaving an opening for stuffing, join the squares by working Blanket Stitches (6 strands) around the edges. Stuff the mat with the rice and cloves; work Blanket Stitches to close the opening.

Fleece Mittens

- fleece mittens • tracing paper
- felt • embroidery floss
- assorted buttons

Trace the patterns (page 154). Using the patterns, cut the designs from felt. Place a piece of cardboard in each mitten (to keep you from stitching completely through the mitten). Pin the felt pieces to the mittens. Use 3 strands of floss to work Blanket Stitches (page 141) for the outlines. Add Stem Stitch arms and French Knot, Satin Stitch, and Cross Stitch details to the snowmen. Sew buttons to the mittens.

Etched Nativity Shade

- 8½"h glass hurricane shade • clear self-adhesive laminate
- craft knife • Delta™ Perm Enamel Surface Conditioner
- Delta™ Perm Enamel White Frost Glass Etching Paint
- 4"h candle

1. Wash the hurricane shade with soapy water; rinse well and dry thoroughly.
2. For the bottom portion of the scene, cut a piece of laminate to fit around the bottom half of the shade. Cut a gentle wave pattern along the top edge of the paper; adhere to the shade.
3. Trace the pattern (page 155) onto the plastic side of another piece of laminate. Remove the paper backing a bit at a time and position it on the shade, slightly overlapping the top edge of the first piece of laminate. Use a craft knife to carefully cut around the designs; remove the excess paper (the background).
4. Follow the manufacturer's instructions to apply the surface conditioner and etching paint. Remove the laminate after 2 hours. Use a needle to scratch the halo and star rays in the etching paint. Place the shade over the candle.

Never leave burning candles unattended.

Fleece Mittens

Personalized Dog Treat Jar

- jar with tight fitting lid • vinyl fabric • transfer paper
- acrylic paint and paintbrush • brush-on clear acrylic sealer
- removable double-sided tape • scoop • chalk • assorted ribbons • cardstock • rub-on holiday message

1. Measure around the jar; add $1^1/_4$". Cut a piece of vinyl that length and about $2/_3$ of the jar's height.
2. Using your computer, print out the dog's name (in a personality-appropriate font). Transfer the name to the center front of the vinyl rectangle; paint. Brush the painted part only with the sealer.
3. Topstitch close to the top and bottom edges of the vinyl rectangle. Overlapping the short ends about $1/_2$", sew the vinyl rectangle together, forming a ring. Place the vinyl ring on the jar.
4. To make the scoop pocket, place tape on the outside of the scoop and wrap a piece of vinyl around it. Draw the shape of the scoop on the wrong side of the vinyl with chalk. Remove the scoop and cut the pocket about $1/_4$" outside the drawn line, cutting straight across the top.
5. Place the vinyl pocket on the scoop again. Hold the scoop and the pocket on the jar in the desired position. Mark the position of the pocket on the vinyl ring with chalk. Remove the ring from the jar and the scoop from the pocket. Sew the pocket onto the ring, following the placement markings.
6. Place the ring on the jar; then add a bow and a layered cardstock gift tag with a rub-on message to the scoop. Place the scoop in the pocket and add doggie treats or kibble.

"Chocolate" Dipped Dog Treats

1	cup water
$1/_2$	cup peanut butter
2	tablespoons vegetable oil
2	cups all-purpose flour
$1/_2$	cup wheat germ
12	ounces vanilla candy coating, chopped
6	ounces carob chips

In a medium bowl, combine water, peanut butter, and vegetable oil; mix until smooth. Stir in flour and wheat germ. On a lightly floured surface, roll out dough to $1/_4$" thickness. Use a $1^1/_2$" x $2^1/_2$" dog bone-shaped cookie cutter to cut out treats. Place on an ungreased baking sheet. Bake at 350° for 18 to 20 minutes or until tops are lightly brown. Cool on a wire rack. In medium bowl, melt candy coating in microwave. Dip treats halfway into candy coating; place on a wire rack until candy coating hardens. In a small bowl, melt carob chips in microwave; stir until smooth. Drizzle over candy coating; allow to harden. Store in an airtight container.
Yield: about $3^1/_2$ dozen dog treats

Personalized Dog Treat Jar

"Chocolate" Dipped Dog Treats

Fig. 1

Fig. 2
colored with pastels   *not colored*

Fig. 3
completely colored

Pet Portraits

- frame (with opening 8" x 10" or smaller and mat
- digital or scanned photo of pet • color printer • matte finish white cardstock • artist's pastels • clear acrylic spray sealer

Print out several copies of the photo on cardstock so you can experiment with strokes and techniques using the pastels.

1. Size the photo (page 142) to fit your mat. Cut the cardstock to 8½" x 11". Print the photo, in color, on the cardstock.
2. Use pastels to enhance the photo with strokes of color, highlighting the desired areas and covering up any unwanted backgrounds. It is not important to completely cover the photo, but rather to enhance the photo with pastel strokes for a painted portrait look (Figs. 1-3).
3. Working in a well-ventilated area, spray the portrait with 2 light coats of sealer. Trim to fit the mat.

Elf Costume

- green felt • 13 jingle bells • ⅛"w ribbon • fabric glue
- elastic cord • silk holly leaves

1. Measure the dog's neck; add 2" and divide by 4. Divide this measurement by 2.75. Multiply the result by 100 and photocopy the pattern (page 154) at this percentage. Fold the felt into ¼'s, with the folds at the top and left. Matching the fold lines of the pattern to the folds of the felt, cut the collar. Cut along one fold.
2. Sew a bell to each collar point. Tie a bow above each bell.
3. Leaving long tails to tie the collar around the dog's neck, sew ribbon along the neck edge of the collar.
4. Cut a square of felt for the hat (we used a 12" square). Overlapping to fit the dog's head, glue 2 adjacent edges together, forming a pointed cone. Turn the bottom point up to make the hat brim. Sew the ends of an elastic cord length to the bottom sides of the hat.
5. Attach holly leaves and a bell to the top of the hat. Add a ribbon bow.

Catnip Stockings

- felt • pinking shears • embroidery floss • catnip
- fabric glue • ribbon • cardstock • decorative-edged scissors • hole punch

1. Reduce the patterns (page 152) to 70%; cut out. Draw around the stocking pattern on one piece of felt; do not cut out. Using the patterns, cut the cuff and snowflakes from felt, using pinking shears to cut the snowflakes.
2. Using 3 strands of floss, work Straight Stitches (page 141) to attach each snowflake to the drawn stocking.
3. Place 2 felt pieces together with the decorated stocking on top. Leaving the top open, stitch along the drawn line. Cut the stocking about ¼" outside the sewn line.
4. Place catnip in the stocking. Sew the cuff to the top of the stocking, stitching through all layers to close the stocking. Glue a bow to the stocking
5. Write "Meow-y Christmas!" on a layered cardstock tag. Punch a hole and use floss to tie the tag to the bow.

Elf Costume

Catnip Stockings

Cat Snuggle Pillow

• wool fabric • coordinating fabric • polyester fiberfill

For all sewing, match the right sides and use a ¹/₂" seam allowance.

1. Cut a 19" square each from wool and coordinating fabric for the pillow. Cut a 19" x 16" piece each from wool and coordinating fabric for the flap.

2. Sew the flap pieces together along one long edge. Turn right side out and press. Topstitch along the sewn edge. Baste along the remaining edges through both layers.

3. Place the flap, wool side down, on the right side of the wool pillow piece, matching the raw edges. Layer the coordinating fabric pillow piece on top; pin. Sew the pieces together, leaving an opening for turning. Press the seam allowances open. Matching seams, flatten each corner and sew across it 1¹/₂" from the point to create a boxed corner. Trim excess fabric at the corners.

4. Turn right side out and lightly stuff the pillow. Sew the opening closed.

creating fun *food gifts* for the HOLIDAYS

Whether baked or blended, savory or sweet—

these *treats* are one-size-fits-all!

For each name on your list, you'll find a

perfectly tasteful present

that's lovingly bagged, boxed,

or nestled in a basket for *gift-giving*.

❄

Tea-Lover's Basket

• 2 tea containers • scrapbook paper, ribbons, rub-on letters, and acrylic jewels • assorted beads and a teacup charm • head pins • round-nose jewelry pliers • jewelry chains • jump rings • mailing tag • craft glue • hole punch • basket • place mat • iridescent shredded basket filler • teapot, infuser, and sugar crystal stir sticks • ribbon bow

1. Fill tea containers with Orange-Spice Tea and Chamomile-Vanilla Tea. Decorate scrapbook paper tags with ribbon, rub-on letters, and jewels. Add a tag to each container.
2. For each bead dangle on the infuser, thread beads onto a head pin. Use pliers to make an eye loop (page 142), connecting the head pin to a chain. Use a jump ring (page 142) to attach the chain to the infuser. Use jump rings to attach the charm to a chain and then to the infuser.
3. Cover the mailing tag with scrapbook paper; punch a hole near the top. Knot ribbons through the hole and attach the infuser.
4. Tie stir sticks together with ribbon.
5. Line the basket with the place mat and filler. Add the teapot, tea containers, infuser, and stir sticks, along with a pretty bow.

Orange-Spice Tea

- 1 tablespoon loose tea
- 1 teaspoon dried orange peel
- 1 teaspoon whole cloves
- 1 teaspoon whole allspice
- 1 cinnamon stick, broken into 3 pieces

Combine all ingredients. Store in an airtight container. Give with serving instructions. **Yield:** 6 teaspoons tea mix

To serve: Place 2 teaspoons of tea mix into an infuser in a teacup. Add boiling water and allow to steep 3 to 4 minutes. Remove infuser.

Chamomile-Vanilla Tea

- 1 tablespoon loose tea
- 2 tablespoons chamomile, crushed
- 1 vanilla bean, cut into small pieces

Combine all ingredients. Store in an airtight container. Give with serving instructions. **Yield:** 6 teaspoons tea mix

To serve: Place 2 teaspoons of tea mix into an infuser in a teacup. Add boiling water and allow to steep 3 to 4 minutes. Remove infuser.

Orange-Spice Tea

Chamomile-Vanilla Tea

Tea-Lover's Basket

Cinnamon Mocha Mix

- 1 jar (16 ounces) non-dairy powdered creamer
- 1 package (16 ounces) chocolate mix for milk
- 1 package (16 ounces) confectioners sugar
- 6 cups nonfat dry milk powder
- 1/2 cup cocoa
- 1/4 cup instant coffee granules
- 2 teaspoons ground cinnamon

In a very large bowl, combine creamer, chocolate mix, confectioners sugar, dry milk, cocoa, coffee granules, and cinnamon. Store in an airtight container. Place 2 cups of mix into a resealable food bag and give with serving instructions. **Yield:** about 14 cups mix

To serve: Pour 6 ounces hot water over 2$\frac{1}{2}$ heaping tablespoons mocha mix; stir until well blended. Serve hot.

Ribbon-Wrapped Bag

- cardstock • scrapbook paper
- decorative-edged scissors
- double-sided tape • rub-on letters • snowflake rubber stamp • ink pad • glitter glue
- bagged Cinnamon Mocha Mix
- small white paper bag
- ribbon • snowflake charm
- mini clip

1. For the tag, cut and layer 2 pieces of cardstock onto a piece of scrapbook paper. Add rub-on words and stamp snowflakes around the letters. Highlight the snowflakes with glitter glue.
2. Place the bagged Cinnamon Mocha Mix in the paper bag. Fold the top of the bag about 2" to the back and tape closed. Wrap ribbon around the bag, leaving about 2" extra coming over the top of the bag from the back; tape the ribbon in place.
3. Tape the tag to the bag front. Bring the ribbon from the back over the front; trim the end. Clip the charm and the ribbon to the top of the bag.

Cinnamon Mocha Mix
Ribbon-Wrapped Bag

Mexican Cheese Crackers
Seasoned Pretzels
Italian Cracker Snacks

Mexican Cheese Crackers

- 1 box (14¹/₂ ounces) cheese crackers
- ¹/₂ cup butter or margarine, melted
- 1 package taco seasoning mix
- 1 tablespoon Worcestershire sauce
- ¹/₂ teaspoon seasoned salt

Place crackers in a large shallow baking pan. In a small bowl, combine butter, taco seasoning mix, Worcestershire, and salt. Pour butter mixture over crackers; stir well. Bake at 250° for 1 hour, stirring every 15 minutes. Pour onto waxed paper to cool. Store in an airtight container.
Yield: about 6 cups of snack mix

Seasoned Pretzels

- 6 cups pretzels (use different shapes, if desired)
- ¹/₂ cup butter or margarine, melted
- 1 package ranch-style dip mix
- 1 tablespoon Worcestershire sauce
- ¹/₂ teaspoon seasoned salt

Place pretzels in a large shallow baking pan. In a small bowl, combine butter, dip mix, Worcestershire, and salt. Pour butter mixture over pretzels; stir well. Bake at 250° for 1 hour, stirring every 15 minutes. Pour onto waxed paper to cool. Store in an airtight container.
Yield: 6 cups of snack mix

Italian Cracker Snacks

- 1 box (9 ounces) round butter-flavor mini crackers
- ¹/₄ cup butter or margarine, melted
- 1 package zesty Italian salad dressing mix
- 1 tablespoon Worcestershire sauce
- ¹/₄ teaspoon seasoned salt

Place crackers in a large shallow baking pan. In a small bowl, combine butter, salad dressing mix, Worcestershire, and salt. Pour butter mixture over crackers; stir well. Bake at 250° for 1 hour, stirring every 15 minutes. Pour onto waxed paper to cool. Store in an airtight container.
Yield: about 4 cups of snack mix

*Dried Bean Soup
& Seasoning
Mixes*

Seasonings

Seasoning Tag

Dried Bean Soup & Seasoning Mixes

Dried Bean Soup Mix

$1/2$ cup of *each* of the following:
kidney beans, yellow split peas, black beans, red lentils, small red beans, and green split peas

Seasoning Mix

  1 tablespoon dried sweet pepper flakes
  2 teaspoons chicken bouillon granules
  2 teaspoons dried minced onion
$1^{1}/2$ teaspoons salt
  1 teaspoon dried parsley flakes
$1/2$ teaspoon ground black pepper
$1/2$ teaspoon garlic powder
$1/2$ teaspoon celery seed

For dried bean mix, layer beans in a clear gift container.

For seasoning mix, combine all ingredients. Place in the center of a plastic wrap square; tie closed with raffia. Give with recipe for Seasoned Bean Soup.

Yield: about 3 cups dried bean mix and about $1/4$ cup seasoning mix

Seasoned Bean Soup

  Dried Bean Mix (3 cups)
  2 cans ($14^{1}/2$ ounces each) stewed tomatoes
  Seasoning Mix ($1/4$ cup)

Rinse beans and place in a large Dutch oven. Pour 4 cups boiling water over beans; cover and let soak overnight.

Drain beans and return to Dutch oven. Add 6 cups water, cover, and bring to a boil over high heat. Reduce heat to low and simmer 1 to $1^{1}/2$ hours or until beans are almost tender. Add tomatoes and seasoning mix. Stirring occasionally, cover and simmer 30 minutes. Uncover beans and continue to simmer about 1 hour longer or until beans are tender and soup thickens. Serve warm.

Yield: about 10 cups soup

Bay Seafood Seasoning

Five-Spice Powder

Greek Seasoning

Creole Seasoning

Herbs Seasoning

Ground Seasoning

Herbs Seasoning

1 tablespoon ground thyme
1 tablespoon dried oregano leaves
2 teaspoons rubbed sage
1 teaspoon dried rosemary leaves
1 teaspoon dried marjoram leaves
1 teaspoon dried basil leaves
1 teaspoon dried parsley flakes

Process all ingredients in a food processor until well blended. Store in an airtight container. Use seasoning in omelets or with fish, vegetables, or chicken.
Yield: about $1/4$ cup seasoning

Creole Seasoning

1 tablespoon salt
$1^{1}/_{2}$ teaspoons garlic powder
$1^{1}/_{2}$ teaspoons onion powder
$1^{1}/_{2}$ teaspoons paprika
$1^{1}/_{4}$ teaspoons dried thyme leaves
1 teaspoon ground red pepper
$3/_{4}$ teaspoon ground black pepper
$3/_{4}$ teaspoon dried oregano leaves
$1/_{2}$ teaspoon crushed bay leaf
$1/_{4}$ teaspoon chili powder

Process all ingredients in a food processor until well blended. Store in an airtight container. Use seasoning with seafood, chicken, beef, or vegetables.
Yield: about $1/4$ cup seasoning

Greek Seasoning

2 teaspoons salt
2 teaspoons ground oregano
$1^{1}/_{2}$ teaspoons onion powder
$1^{1}/_{2}$ teaspoons garlic powder
1 teaspoon cornstarch
1 teaspoon ground black pepper
1 teaspoon beef bouillon granules
1 teaspoon dried parsley flakes
$1/_{2}$ teaspoon ground cinnamon
$1/_{2}$ teaspoon ground nutmeg

Process all ingredients in a food processor until well blended. Store in an airtight container. Use seasoning with steaks, pork chops, chicken, or fish.
Yield: about $1/4$ cup seasoning

Five-Spice Powder

2 teaspoons anise seeds, crushed
2 teaspoons ground black pepper
2 teaspoons fennel seeds, crushed
2 teaspoons ground cloves
2 teaspoons ground cinnamon
$1^{1}/_{2}$ teaspoons ground ginger
$1/_{2}$ teaspoon ground allspice

Combine all ingredients; store in an airtight container. Use with fish or pork.
Yield: about $1/4$ cup seasoning

Bay Seafood Seasoning

1 tablespoon crushed bay leaves
$2^{1}/_{2}$ teaspoons celery salt
$1^{1}/_{2}$ teaspoons dry mustard
$1^{1}/_{2}$ teaspoons ground black pepper
$3/_{4}$ teaspoon ground nutmeg
$1/_{2}$ teaspoon ground cloves
$1/_{2}$ teaspoon ground ginger
$1/_{2}$ teaspoon paprika
$1/_{2}$ teaspoon ground red pepper
$1/_{4}$ teaspoon ground mace
$1/_{4}$ teaspoon ground cardamom

Process all ingredients in a food processor until well blended. Store in an airtight container. Use seasoning with seafood or chicken.
Yield: about $1/4$ cup seasoning

Ground Seasoning

2 tablespoons celery seed
1 tablespoon onion powder
1 tablespoon salt

Process all ingredients in a food processor until well blended. Store in an airtight container. Use seasoning in stews, chowders, or sandwich spreads.
Yield: about $1/4$ cup seasoning

Seasoning Tag instructions on page 83

Creamy Mocha Liqueur

Embossed Velvet Gift Bag

Pecan Mini Muffins

- 1 cup firmly packed brown sugar
- 1/2 cup butter or margarine, melted
- 2 large eggs
- 1 teaspoon vanilla extract
- 1 cup chopped pecans
- 1/2 cup all-purpose flour

Combine first 4 ingredients in a bowl, beating with a wire whisk until smooth. Stir in pecans and flour. Place paper baking cups in miniature (1³/₄") muffin pans; spoon 1 tablespoon batter into each cup. Bake at 375° for 12 minutes or until lightly browned. Cool in pans on wire racks. **Yield:** 3 dozen mini muffins

Mini Muffin Bag & Tag
instructions on page 85

White Chocolate-Macadamia Nut Muffins

- 2¹/₂ cups biscuit mix
- 1/2 cup sugar
- 3/4 cup coarsely chopped white chocolate
- 1/2 cup coarsely chopped macadamia nuts
- 3/4 cup half-and-half
- 3 tablespoons vegetable oil
- 2 teaspoons vanilla extract
- 1 large egg, lightly beaten

Combine biscuit mix and sugar in a large bowl; stir in chocolate and nuts. Make a well in center of mixture. Combine half-and-half and remaining 3 ingredients; add to dry ingredients, stirring just until dry ingredients are moistened. Spoon into 6 (3¹/₂" x 1³/₄") greased muffin pans, filling two-thirds full. Bake at 400° for 15 to 18 minutes or until a wooden pick inserted into center comes out clean. Remove from pans immediately. **Yield:** ¹/₂ dozen muffins

Creamy Mocha Liqueur

- 1 can (14 ounces) sweetened condensed milk
- 1 cup whipping cream
- 1 cup coffee-flavored liqueur
- 1/2 cup chocolate-flavored liqueur

Pour sweetened condensed milk, whipping cream, and liqueurs in a blender. Process until blended. Pour into gift bottle. Store in refrigerator. Serve chilled. **Yield:** about 3²/₃ cups liqueur

Embossed Velvet Gift Bag
instructions on page 85

Painted Mug with Tag
instructions on page 84

Chocolate Pinwheel Loaves

- 1/2 cup milk
- 1/4 cup butter or margarine
- 1/4 cup sugar
- 3/4 teaspoon salt
- 1 package active dry yeast
- 1/4 cup warm water (105° to 115°)
- 2 large eggs, beaten
- 3 to 3 1/4 cups all-purpose flour
- 1 square (1 ounce) unsweetened chocolate, melted and cooled
- Glaze

Combine first 4 ingredients in a saucepan; heat until butter melts. Remove from heat, and cool to 105° to 115°. Combine yeast and warm water in a 1-cup liquid measuring cup; let stand 5 minutes. Combine yeast mixture, liquid mixture, eggs, and 2 cups flour in a large mixing bowl; beat at medium speed with an electric mixer until smooth. Transfer half of mixture to a second bowl. Beat melted chocolate into one portion of mixture. Stir enough remaining flour into each portion to make a soft dough. Knead each portion of dough on a floured surface until smooth and elastic (8 to 10 minutes). Place each in a well-greased bowl, turning to grease top. Cover and let rise in a warm place (85°), free from drafts, 45 minutes or until doubled in bulk.

Punch each dough down and turn out onto a floured surface; roll each into an 18" x 10" rectangle. Position chocolate dough on top of plain dough. Cut dough in half to make two 10" x 9" pieces. Roll each piece, jellyroll fashion, starting at short end. Pinch seams and ends together; fold ends under. Place, seam-side down, in 2 greased 8 1/2" x 4 1/2" loaf pans. Cover and let rise in a warm place, free from drafts, 45 minutes or until doubled in bulk.

Bake at 350° for 20 minutes or until loaves are golden. Remove from pans; place on a wire rack. Drizzle Glaze over warm loaves. Serve warm or cool.
Yield: 2 loaves

Glaze

- 1 cup confectioners sugar
- 1 1/2 tablespoons milk
- 1/2 teaspoon vanilla extract

Combine all ingredients, stirring well.
Yield: about 1/3 cup glaze

White Chocolate-Macadamia Nut Muffins

Painted Mug with Tag

Pecan Mini Muffins

Mini Muffin Bag & Tag

Chocolate Pinwheel Loaves

Fabric & Paper Bags

Fabric & Paper Bags instructions on pages 83 & 84

Peanut Butter Crumb Cookies

- 1 cup butter or margarine, softened
- 1 cup extra-crunchy peanut butter
- 3/4 cup firmly packed brown sugar
- 3/4 cup granulated sugar
- 2 eggs
- 1 1/2 teaspoons vanilla extract
- 2 1/2 cups all-purpose flour
- 1 teaspoon baking powder
- 1 teaspoon baking soda
- 1/2 teaspoon salt
- 1 1/2 cups coarsely crushed cinnamon graham crackers (about 22 rectangles), divided
- 1/2 cup finely chopped dry-roasted peanuts

In a large bowl, cream butter, peanut butter, and sugars until fluffy. Add eggs and vanilla; beat until smooth. In a medium bowl, combine flour, baking powder, baking soda, and salt. Add dry ingredients to creamed mixture; beat until well blended. Stir in 1 cup cracker crumbs. In a small bowl, combine remaining 1/2 cup cracker crumbs and peanuts. Roll heaping teaspoonfuls of dough into balls; roll in crumb mixture. Place balls on a lightly greased baking sheet; flatten with a fork. Bake at 350° for 7 to 9 minutes or until lightly browned. Transfer to a wire rack to cool. Store in an airtight container. **Yield:** about 7 dozen cookies

Peanut Butter Crumb Cookies

Tree Gift Bags

Tree Gift Bags

- paper-backed fusible web
- gold and green fabrics
- poster board • wrapped Peanut Butter Crumb Cookies
- white lunch-size paper bags
- craft glue

1. For each bag, trace the patterns (page 156) on the paper side of the web, leaving about 1/2" between the pieces. Cut out slightly outside the drawn lines. Fuse the appliqués to the wrong side of the fabric, then to the poster board; cut out the pieces.
2. Overlapping sections about 1/4", glue the sections to the front of the bag, leaving the scalloped edges unglued. Glue the star to the tree top.
3. Place the Peanut Butter Crumb Cookies in the bag. Fold the bag top about 2" to the back. Fold the top corners back to form a point; glue to secure.

Fruited Rice Mix

- 5 cups uncooked wild and whole grain brown rice blend
- 1³/₄ cups chopped dried apples
- 1 cup golden raisins
- ¹/₂ cup toasted slivered almonds
- 6 tablespoons instant chicken bouillon
- 5 tablespoons dried minced onion
- 1 tablespoon curry powder
- 2 teaspoons salt

Combine all ingredients, mixing well. Store in an airtight container in refrigerator. Mixture may be stored in refrigerator up to one month. Give with serving instructions.
Yield: about 9¹/₂ cups mix

To serve: Keep rice mix refrigerated until ready to prepare. In a heavy 2-quart saucepan, combine contents of bag (1 cup), 2 cups water, and 2 tablespoons butter. Bring to a boil, cover, and reduce heat to medium low. Simmer 45 to 55 minutes or until water is absorbed. Turn off heat and allow to sit, covered, for 10 minutes.
Yield: 1¹/₂ cups cooked rice

Fruited Rice Mix

Rice Mix Bags

Rice Mix Bags

• cardstock • embellishments for tags (we used scrapbook paper; rub-on letters, words, and images; as well as glitter glue) • disposable cake decorating bags • Fruited Rice Mix • assorted ribbons and trims • large paper clips • jingle bells

Photocopy the recipe on page 158; cut out and attach to the back of a cardstock tag. Embellish the tag front. Fill each disposable bag with 1 cup of the Fruited Rice Mix. Fold and tape the bag top closed. Tie ribbons and trims to a paper clip and attach the tag and a bell to the rice-filled bag.

Monogram Cookies

- ½ cup butter, softened
- 1 cup confectioners sugar
- 1 egg
- ½ teaspoon almond extract
- 1 cup all-purpose flour
- 6 tablespoons cocoa
- ¼ teaspoon salt
  Chipboard letter
  Windowed box for
    cookies (ours is
    4½" x 5½" x 1½")

In a large bowl, beat butter and confectioners sugar until fluffy. Add egg and almond extract; beat until smooth. In a small bowl, combine flour, cocoa, and salt. Add dry ingredients to creamed mixture; stir until a soft dough forms.

Divide dough in half. Wrap in plastic wrap and chill 1 hour.

On a lightly floured surface, use a floured rolling pin to roll out half of dough to ¼" thickness. Enlarge the chipboard letter to fit in box. Use this template and a sharp knife to cut out cookies. Transfer to an ungreased baking sheet. Bake at 375° for 5 to 7 minutes or until bottoms are lightly browned. Transfer cookies to a wire rack to cool. Repeat with remaining dough. Place 2 cookies in the windowed box. Store remaining cookies in an airtight container.
Yield: about 8 (3½"w x 4"h) cookies

Special Couple's Gift

- large candle holder or vase (ours is 9" dia. x 8½"h)
- scrapbook paper • shredded basket filler • 2 napkins • box of Monogram Cookies • ribbon
- chipboard letter used to make cookie template • tinsel spray
- adhesive foam dots • taper candles • champagne or wine
- champagne glasses • assorted greenery

1. Line the hurricane glass with scrapbook paper. Fill with basket filler. Add napkins toward the back of the hurricane.
2. Wrap the box of Monogram Cookies with a scrapbook paper and ribbon band. Add the couple's monogram chipboard letter and a few tinsel spray pieces to the box with foam dots.
3. Place the candles, champagne, glasses, and cookie box in the hurricane. Fill in with greenery and tinsel spray.

Monogram Cookies

Special Couple's Gift

Butter Crunch Pretzels
Santa Bag

Lemon-Ginger
Liqueur

Butter Crunch Pretzels

- 16   cups small pretzel twists
- 1   cup firmly packed brown sugar
- 1/2   cup butter or margarine
- 1/4   cup light corn syrup
- 1   teaspoon vanilla-butter-nut flavoring
- 1/2   teaspoon baking soda

Place pretzels in a large roasting pan. Butter sides of a heavy medium saucepan. Combine brown sugar, butter, and corn syrup in saucepan. Stirring constantly, cook over medium-low heat until sugar dissolves. Increase heat to medium and bring to a boil. Cook, without stirring, 5 minutes. Remove from heat. Stir in vanilla-butter-nut flavoring and baking soda (syrup will foam). Pour syrup over pretzels; stir until pretzels are well coated. Bake at 200° for 1 hour, stirring every 15 minutes. Spread on greased aluminum foil to cool. Store in an airtight container.

Yield: about 20 cups pretzels

Santa Bag instructions on page 86

Lemon-Ginger Liqueur

- 4   lemons
- 1   bottle (750 ml) vodka
- 1/4   teaspoon ground ginger
- 1 1/2   cups superfine sugar

Peel zest (yellow portion) from lemons. Combine vodka, lemon zest, and ginger in a 1-quart airtight container. Let stand in a cool place 24 hours. Strain and discard lemon zest from vodka. Add sugar to vodka; stir until sugar dissolves. Let stand 1 month at room temperature. Pour into a gift container.

Yield: about 4 cups liqueur

Snowball Cupcakes

1 package (18.25 ounces) yellow cake mix
3 eggs
$^{1}/_{3}$ cup vegetable oil
1 can (8$^{1}/_{2}$ ounces) cream of coconut
1 cup sour cream
1 container (12 ounces) white frosting
1$^{3}/_{4}$ cups sweetened shredded coconut
Candied cherry halves to decorate

Combine cake mix, eggs, and oil in a large bowl; beat until well blended. Add cream of coconut and sour cream; beat until smooth. Line muffin pan with aluminum foil muffin cups; fill cups half full. Bake at 350° for 16 to 18 minutes or until a toothpick inserted in center of cupcake comes out clean. Cool in pan on a wire rack.

Spread frosting on tops of cupcakes. Sprinkle with coconut. Decorate with candied cherry halves. Store in a single layer in an airtight container.
Yield: about 3 dozen cupcakes

Handy Mitten Wraps

• tracing paper • medium-weight cardboard • spray adhesive • fabric • craft glue • ribbon for mitten cuff • clear cellophane • curling ribbon

Trace the pattern (page 157). For each Mitten Wrap, use the pattern and cut a mitten from cardboard. Working in a well-ventilated area, use spray adhesive to adhere the mitten to the wrong side of the fabric. Trim excess fabric, leaving about $^{3}/_{4}$" fabric beyond the cardboard. Clipping as necessary, wrap and glue the fabric to the back of the mitten. Glue ribbon to the mitten cuff, wrapping and gluing the ends to the back. Center the mitten and cupcake on a 20" cellophane square. Gather the cellophane over the cupcake and tie with curling ribbon. Curl the ribbon ends.

Snowball Cupcakes
Handy Mitten Wraps

Graham Cracker Houses

Graham Cracker Houses

• graham crackers • purchased white decorating tube icing • variety of candy items to decorate houses

Use icing to "glue" pieces together. Refer to drawings when cutting and gluing.

1. For the front wall, cut the top corners from 1 cracker half. Repeat for the back wall.
2. Glue the front and back walls to 1 cracker half (base). Use props to hold the walls upright until the side walls are added.
3. For the side walls, glue 2 cracker quarters to the base and front and back walls. Allow icing to harden slightly.
4. For the roof, apply icing to the top edges of the walls. Place 2 cracker halves on top of the house. Apply icing along the peak of the roof. Allow icing to harden for several hours or overnight before decorating.
5. Use icing to attach candies to the house for doors, windows, shutters, chimneys, fences, shrubbery, and roof. Allow icing to harden.
6. Store each house in an airtight container until ready to give.

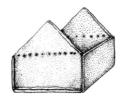

Christmas Dipped Cookies

- 6 ounces chocolate candy coating
- 6 ounces vanilla candy coating
- 1 package (16 ounces) chocolate sandwich cookies

    Purchased red, green, and white decorating tube icing

Melt chocolate and vanilla candy coating in separate small saucepans following package directions. Using tongs, dip half of cookies into chocolate and remaining cookies into vanilla. Place on a wire rack to harden. Use decorating icing to decorate cookies. Allow icing to harden. Store in an airtight container.

Yield: about 3¹/₂ dozen cookies

Joy Tin

• 6¹/₂" dia. lidded tin • spray paints • tracing paper • transfer paper • acrylic paints and paintbrushes • clear acrylic spray sealer

Working in a well-ventilated area, spray paint the outside of the tin and the lid. Trace the pattern (page 156). Transfer the pattern to the tin lid and paint the design. Paint stripes on the side of the tin. Spray the outside of the tin and the lid with acrylic sealer.

Christmas Candy Canes

- 4 ounces chocolate candy coating
- 4 ounces vanilla candy coating
- 2 dozen small peppermint candy canes
- 1 cup confectioners sugar
- 1 tablespoon milk

    Red and green paste food coloring

Melt chocolate and vanilla candy coating in separate small saucepans following package directions. Using tongs, dip half of candy canes into chocolate and remaining candy canes into vanilla. Place on a wire rack to harden.

For icing, combine sugar and milk in a small bowl, stirring until smooth. Divide icing in half. Tint one half red and one half green. Drizzle icing over candy canes. Allow icing to harden. Store in an airtight container.

Yield: 2 dozen candy canes

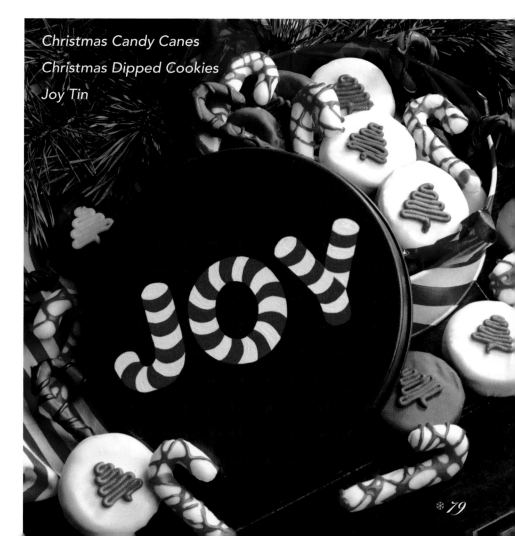

Christmas Candy Canes

Christmas Dipped Cookies

Joy Tin

Lemon-Date Muffin Mix

- 12 cups all-purpose baking mix, divided
- 3 cups sugar, divided
- 3 teaspoons baking soda, divided
- 1½ cups butter, divided
- 3 teaspoons lemon extract, divided
- 2 packages (8 ounces each) chopped dates

Process 6 cups baking mix, 1½ cups sugar, and 1½ teaspoons baking soda in a large food processor until blended. Add ¾ cup butter and 1½ teaspoons lemon extract; process until blended. Add 1 package dates and pulse process just until mixed. Divide muffin mix into 3 resealable plastic bags. Repeat with remaining ingredients. Give with baking instructions.
Yield: 6 bags muffin mix, about 3 cups each

To bake: Line a muffin pan with paper muffin cups. In a large bowl, combine 1 bag muffin mix, 8 ounces lemon yogurt, and 1 egg; stir until just moistened. Spoon batter into muffin cups, filling each about two-thirds full. Sprinkle ¼ teaspoon sugar over each muffin. Bake at 400° for 15 to 17 minutes or until tops are lightly browned. Serve warm or transfer to a wire rack to cool. Store in an airtight container.
Yield: about 1 dozen muffins

Spoon Santa Sacks

- wooden spoons • acrylic paints and paintbrush • black permanent marker • glossy wood-tone spray • clear acrylic sealer • hot glue gun • buttons • brown lunch-size paper bags • bagged Lemon-Date Muffin Mix • ribbon • floral greenery clusters • jingle bells

1. For each sack, freehand draw Santa's face on the bowl of a spoon.
2. Paint Santa's face. Paint the handle and the back of the spoon red. Use the marker to color the eyes and draw the outlines and details on Santa. Working in a well-ventilated area, spray the spoon lightly with wood-tone spray, then sealer. Glue a button to the end of the handle.
3. Place a bag of Lemon-Date Muffin Mix and the baking instructions in a paper bag and fold the top about 2½" to the front.
4. Cut 2 vertical slits about 1" apart through the front flap and the bag. Thread a length of ribbon through the slits. Knot the ends around the Santa spoon and add a multi-loop bow.
5. Glue a bell and a greenery cluster to the bow.

Lemon-Date Muffin Mix
Spoon Santa Sacks

Aunt Velma's Cranberry-Orange Bread

- 2 cups all-purpose flour
- 1 cup sugar
- 1$\frac{1}{2}$ teaspoons baking powder
- 1 teaspoon baking soda
- $\frac{1}{2}$ teaspoon salt
- 1 cup chopped fresh cranberries
- 1 cup chopped pecans
- $\frac{3}{4}$ cup boiling water
- 2 tablespoons shortening
- $\frac{1}{2}$ cup orange juice
- 1 egg, beaten
- 1 tablespoon orange zest

Combine flour, sugar, baking powder, baking soda, and salt in a large bowl; stir in cranberries and pecans. Set aside.

In a small bowl, combine boiling water and shortening, stirring until shortening dissolves; set aside.

In another small bowl, combine orange juice, egg, and zest. Alternately add shortening and orange juice mixtures to dry ingredients, stirring until well blended. Pour into three 3" x 5$\frac{1}{2}$" greased loaf pans. Bake at 350° for 35 to 40 minutes or until a toothpick inserted in bread comes out clean. Cool on wire rack 10 minutes and remove from pans.

Yield: 3 bread loaves

Contributed by Susan Hamblin from her great-aunt Velma Roring

Aunt Velma's Cranberry-Orange Bread

Bread Board

Bread Board

- Aunt Velma's Cranberry-Orange Bread • cellophane bag
- double-sided tape • mini bread board • scrapbook paper
- ribbon • circle punches (2 sizes) • rub-on seasonal greeting
- glitter glue
- tinsel sprig

1. Place the bread in the cellophane bag and tape the bag closed. Place the bread on the bread board and wrap with a scrapbook paper and ribbon band.
2. Make a tag from 2 scrapbook paper circles. Add a rub-on greeting and run a thin outline of glitter glue on the tag.
3. Slip the tinsel sprig under the ribbon band and attach the tag.

Coconut Pound Cakes

Coconut Pound Cakes

- 1 package (16 ounces) pound cake mix
- 1 cup sour cream
- 2 eggs
- 1 teaspoon coconut extract
- 1 cup frozen shredded coconut, divided
- 1½ cups sifted confectioners sugar
- 2 tablespoons milk

Combine cake mix, sour cream, eggs, and coconut extract in a medium bowl; beat until well blended. Stir in ³/₄ cup coconut. Spoon into greased and floured cups of a 6-mold fluted tube pan. Bake at 325° for 35 to 40 minutes or until a toothpick inserted in center of cake comes out clean. Cool in pan 5 minutes; invert cakes onto a wire rack with waxed paper underneath. Combine confectioners sugar and milk; stir until smooth. Drizzle glaze over warm cakes. Sprinkle with remaining ¹/₄ cup coconut. Allow glaze to harden. Store in an airtight container.

Yield: six 4" cakes

Christmas Pretzels
Festive Gift Bag

Christmas Pretzels

- 1 tablespoon red coarse decorating sugar
- 1 tablespoon green coarse decorating sugar
- 1 tablespoon white coarse decorating sugar
- 18 ounces vanilla candy coating, chopped
- 1 package (10 ounces) 3"-wide Bavarian-style pretzels

In a small bowl, combine red, green, and white decorating sugars; set aside.

Stirring frequently, melt candy coating in a heavy medium saucepan over low heat. Remove from heat. Working with 6 pretzels at a time, dip each pretzel into candy coating. Transfer pretzels to waxed paper. Sprinkle pretzels with sugar mixture before coating hardens. Store in an airtight container in a cool place.

Yield: about 2 dozen pretzels

Festive Gift Bag instructions on page 86

Seasoning Tag
Shown on page 68

- cellophane bags • Seasoning Mixes • tape • cardstock (solid and patterned) • scallop-edged scissors • ribbons • round paper clips

For each gift, fill a bag with a seasoning mix. Fold and tape the bag top closed. Print (on the computer or by hand) the seasoning name on cardstock. For the tag, cut and layer the cardstock name, solid cardstock, and patterned cardstock. Scallop one end with the scissors. Tie ribbons to a paper clip and attach the tag to the seasoning-filled bag.

Fabric Bag
Shown on page 71

- 13" x 16" fabric piece
- embroidery floss • tiny buttons • fabric and muslin scraps • rubber stamp • ink pad • glossy wood-tone spray
- wrapped Chocolate Pinwheel Loaf • raffia • cardstock
- handmade paper • glue stick

For all sewing, use a 1/2" seam allowance unless otherwise stated.

1. Matching right sides and long edges, fold the large fabric piece in half. Sew the long edges together; press the seam allowances open. With the seam at center back, sew one end closed.
2. Flatten each bottom corner to form a point. Sew across each corner 1" from the point. Turn the bag right side out.

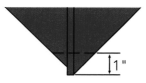

1"

3. For the cuff, fold the top of the bag 1½" to the right side. Spacing evenly and sewing through both layers, use floss to sew buttons to the cuff.
4. Cut a 3½" fabric square and a 3" muslin square; fray the fabric edges. Stamp the design on the muslin square. Working in a well-ventilated area, lightly spray with wood-tone spray and allow to dry.
5. Attach the layered squares to the bag with buttons.
6. Place the loaf in the bag; tie closed with raffia.
7. For the tag, tear squares from cardstock and handmade paper. Stamp the design on the cardstock; spray with wood-tone spray and allow to dry. Layer and glue the squares. Sew a button to the tag; tie the tag to the bag.

Paper Bag
Shown on page 71

• 4 manila tags • thread • green and red handmade papers • 4 red buttons • fabric • spray adhesive • brown paper bag • wrapped Chocolate Pinwheel Loaf • 2 eyelets and an eyelet setter • $1/8$"w ribbon

1. Place 3 tags side-by-side; with one letter on each tag, use a pencil to write "joy" across the tags. Machine stitch over the drawn letters.

2. For each tag, tear 3 holly leaves from green paper. Arrange the leaves on the tags, then sew a vein down the center of each leaf. Sew a button at the center of each set of leaves.
3. Cut a fabric rectangle to fit the front of the bag and fringe the ends. Center and zigzag stitch the fabric piece on a torn red paper rectangle. Working in a well-ventilated area, adhere the rectangle to the bag. Adhere the "joy" tags to the fabric piece.
4. Place the loaf in the bag, then fold the top of the bag 1" to the back. Attach the eyelets through the folded section of the bag. Lace ribbon through the eyelets and tie into a bow.
5. Write a greeting on the gift tag and attach it to the gift.

Painted Mug with Tag
Shown on page 71

• rubber stamps • glass paint and liner paintbrush • ceramic mug • handmade papers • glue stick • ink pad • embroidery floss • 2 jingle bells • packet of specialty coffee or several tea bags • plastic-wrapped White Chocolate-Macadamia Nut Muffin • clear cellophane • raffia

1. Use the stamps and paint to decorate the mug; randomly paint dots on the mug. Touch up the designs with the liner brush and paint if necessary. Follow the paint manufacturer's instructions for curing the paint.
2. For the tag, tear and layer 2 paper squares; stamp the tag. Using floss, sew the bells to the tag. Tie the tag to the mug with raffia.
3. Place the coffee or tea, then the muffin in the mug. Wrap the mug in cellophane and tie with raffia.

Mini Muffin Bag & Tag

Shown on page 71

- fabric • brown paper lunch bag • handmade papers
- embroidery floss • charm
- 4 jingle bells • spray adhesive
- wrapped Pecan Mini Muffins
- rubber stamp • ink pad
- black permanent pen

1. Tear a 1"w fabric strip to fit the width of the bag. Tear paper and fabric pieces to fit the front of the bag.
2. Use floss to sew the charm and 3 bells to the smallest paper piece. Working in a well-ventilated area, layer and adhere the pieces to the bag front.
3. Place a few muffins in the bag. Fold the top of the bag to the front; then adhere the fabric strip to the bag flap.
4. For the tag, layer torn paper rectangles. Personalize the tag with the stamp and pen. Sew the remaining bell to the tag and adhere the tag to the bag.

Embossed Velvet Gift Bag

Shown on page 70

- 19" x 21" piece of 100% rayon velvet • message and motif rubber stamps • fine-point gold paint pen • gold glitter dimensional fabric paint
- bottled Creamy Mocha Liqueur • 2 ornaments • gold cord • greenery sprig

1. To emboss the velvet, place the message stamp, design side up, on a flat surface. Place the velvet, right side down, on the stamp 6" from one short edge of the velvet. Lightly mist the wrong side of the velvet with water. Using a hot, dry iron, press for 10-15 seconds until the impression is made in the velvet. Repeat to emboss the motifs on each side of the message.
2. Draw over the embossed designs on the right side of the velvet with the paint pen. Use dimensional paint to highlight the designs.
3. Matching right sides of the velvet, sew the long edges together with a 1/4" seam allowance. With the seam at the center back, sew across one short edge to form the bottom of the bag. Sew across each corner of the bag 1 1/2" from the ends. Trim the seam allowances to 1/4".

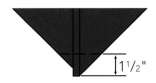

4. Fold the top edge of the bag 3" to the wrong side; topstitch. Turn the bag right side out.
5. Place the bottle in the bag. Thread the ornaments onto the cord and tie a bow around the bag. Tuck greenery under the bow.

Santa Bag
Shown on page 76

- 3¹/₂" x 10" flesh-colored fabric piece • 7" square and 3³/₄" x 10" red fabric pieces
- 10" x 17" white fabric piece
- tracing paper • white and red felt • 2 buttons for eyes • fabric glue • green ribbon • jingle bell • hook and loop fastener square • tracing paper

For all sewing, match the right sides and raw edges and use a ¹/₄" seam allowance.

1. Matching the long edges, sew the flesh-colored fabric piece and 3³/₄" x 10" red fabric piece together; sew the remaining long edge of flesh-colored fabric piece to the white fabric piece.
2. Matching the short ends, fold the pieced fabric in half. Sew the sides of bag together.

3. Flatten and center each side seam against the bottom of the bag; sew across each corner 1¹/₂" from the point (Fig. 1). Turn the bag right side out.

Fig. 1

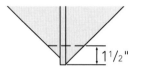

1¹/₂"

4. For the hat, fold two adjacent sides of the red fabric square ¹/₄" to the wrong side; stitch in place. Matching right sides and stitched edges, fold the square in half diagonally. Sew the raw edges together. Turn right side out.
5. Press the top edge of the bag ¹/₄" to the wrong side. Place the open end of the hat along the top back edge of the bag (Fig. 2); baste.

Fig. 2

6. Press the top edge of the bag ¹/₄" to the wrong side again and stitch in place. Sew a bow and bell to the tip of the hat.

7. For the bag closure, center and glue the hook and loop fastener between the inside top edges of the bag.
8. Trace the patterns (page 157) onto tracing paper. Using the patterns, cut the pieces from felt. Glue the felt pieces and buttons to the bag front.

Festive Gift Bag
Shown on page 82

- medium-size gift bag
- clear cellophane • craft glue
- decorative braid • buttons
- ribbons • gold cord to replace bag handles

1. Cut a window in the bag front.
2. Center and glue a cellophane piece inside the bag behind the window.
3. Glue the braid along the edges of the window, the buttons at the corners, and a bow at the top.
4. Replace the bag handles with gold cord.

creating good *food* for the HOLIDAYS

May your Christmases always include

an abundance of *sweet* and *savory* foods!

This collection of kitchen-tested recipes offers something

scrumptious for every holiday meal and get-together.

From appetizers to desserts, you'll find dozens of

new *holiday favorites* here!

❄

Appetizers & Beverages are your chance

to offer something for everyone. Choose from more than a dozen delectable warm or cold drinks. The twelve finger foods include easy spreads and dips, as well as tempting recipes that can be prepared in advance.

Olive Dip

1 cup shredded mozzarella cheese
1 cup shredded sharp Cheddar cheese
1 cup mayonnaise
$3/4$ cup chopped green onions
1 can (5.75 ounces) chopped green olives, drained
1 can (4.25 ounces) chopped black olives
Garnish: green onion tops
Pita chips to serve

Combine all ingredients except garnish and pita chips; spread into a 2-quart baking dish. Bake at 350° for 20 minutes or until mixture is heated through. Garnish, if desired. Serve warm with pita chips.
Yield: 4 cups dip
Contributed by Linda Sunwall

Spinach Appetizers

Shown on page 106

1 cup finely chopped onion
1 cup finely chopped red bell pepper
1 teaspoon minced garlic clove
$1/4$ cup butter
1 package (10 ounces) frozen chopped spinach, thawed and drained
1 cup shredded mozzarella cheese
4 ounces cream cheese
$1/2$ cup sour cream
1 teaspoon salt
2 packages (1.90-ounce package of 15 each) mini phyllo shells

Sauté onion, red bell pepper, and garlic in butter until vegetables are tender. Stir in spinach, mozzarella cheese, and cream cheese; cook until cheese melts. Remove from heat and stir in sour cream and salt, stirring until well blended. Fill each phyllo shell with about 1 tablespoon spinach mixture. Store in an airtight container in refrigerator.
Yield: 30 appetizers

Tasty Ham Spread

1 package (3 ounces) cream cheese, softened
$1/4$ cup mayonnaise
2 cups ground baked ham
2 tablespoons finely chopped sweet pickle
1 tablespoon Dijon mustard
1 teaspoon Worcestershire sauce
Crackers to serve

In a small bowl, beat cream cheese and mayonnaise until well blended. Stir in ham, pickle, mustard, and Worcestershire. Cover and chill 1 hour. Serve ham spread with crackers.
Yield: about 2 cups spread

Irish Cream Fudge
(recipe on page 124)

Olive Dip

Shrimp Cake Appetizers with Remoulade Sauce

These cakes can be made ahead. Fry cakes until slightly browned; drain on paper towels, cover, and refrigerate. When ready to serve, heat cakes under the broiler until both sides are golden brown.

Shrimp Cakes

- 8 ounces cooked and peeled shrimp, finely chopped
- 1/4 cup bread crumbs
- 3 tablespoons mayonnaise
- 1 egg, slightly beaten
- 2 tablespoons all-purpose flour
- 1 tablespoon chopped fresh chives
- 1/2 teaspoon seafood seasoning
- 1/2 teaspoon garlic powder
- 1/2 teaspoon onion powder
- 1/4 teaspoon salt
- 1/4 teaspoon pepper
- 1/2 cup Japenese-style bread crumbs for coating
- 2 tablespoons olive oil, adding more as needed

Remoulade Sauce

- 1 cup mayonnaise
- 2 tablespoons ketchup
- 2 teaspoons Dijon mustard
- 2 teaspoons horseradish
- 1 teaspoon onion powder
- 1/2 teaspoon seafood seasoning
- 1/2 teaspoon garlic powder

For shrimp cakes, combine first 11 ingredients in a medium bowl. Shape mixture into about 1 1/2" diameter patties. Coat with bread crumbs. Fry patties in oil until both sides are golden browned. Drain on paper towels.

For sauce, combine all ingredients. Serve shrimp cakes warm with sauce.

Yield: about 20 shrimp cakes and 1 cup sauce

Roasted Red Pepper-Tomato Bruschetta

    1 jar (7-ounces) roasted red bell peppers,
         drained and cut into short, thin strips
1½ cups ripe tomatoes, seeded and diced
         (about 4 medium tomatoes)
    ¼ cup chopped fresh basil
    3 tablespoons shredded Parmesan cheese
    1 garlic clove, minced
    ½ teaspoon kosher salt
    ¼ teaspoon black pepper
   24 bagette bread slices, toasted
         Garnish: shredded Parmesan cheese,
           cooked bacon pieces

  Combine first 7 ingredients; refrigerate until
ready to serve.
  To serve, spoon 1 heaping tablespoon of
mixture on each bread slice. Garnish, if desired.
Yield: 2 dozen appetizers

Slow Cooker Reuben Dip

Champagne Punch
    2 cups sugar
    2 cups water
    3 cups apple juice
    2 cups pineapple juice
    2 cups apricot nectar juice
1½ cups lemon juice
    1 can (6 ounces) frozen orange juice
    2 quarts ginger ale
    2 bottles (750 ml each) champagne

  Stir together sugar and water in a
saucepan; cook over medium heat until sugar
dissolves and mixture simmers. Remove from
heat; cool. Stir together next 5 ingredients;
add sugar syrup. Chill until ready to serve.
Freeze ginger ale until slushy.
  To serve, pour fruit juice mixture into a
punch bowl; stir in champagne and partially
frozen ginger ale.
Yield: about twenty-six 8-ounce servings

Slow Cooker Reuben Dip
    1 jar (16 ounces) sauerkraut, drained
    3 cups shredded Swiss cheese
    1 package (8 ounces) cream cheese
    ¾ pound deli corned beef, cut into small
         pieces
    ¾ cup Thousand Island dressing
         Toasted party rye cocktail bread to serve

  Combine sauerkraut, cream cheese, Swiss
cheese, corn beef, and dressing in slow cooker.
Cover and cook on low for 2 hours or until mixture
is hot and cheese is melted, stirring occasionally.
Serve with rye cocktail bread.
Yield: about 4 cups dip

Hot Buttered Rum Cordial

Shown on page 132

2 cups apple cider
1/2 cup firmly packed brown sugar
1/4 teaspoon ground cinnamon
1/4 teaspoon ground allspice
2 cups rum
1/4 cup amaretto
1 tablespoon butter-flavored extract

In a small saucepan, combine first 4 ingredients. Stirring constantly, cook over medium heat until sugar dissolves. Remove from heat. Stir in rum, amaretto, and butter-flavored extract. Store in an airtight container in refrigerator 8 hours or overnight to allow flavors to blend.

Strain cordial through cheesecloth or a coffee filter. Reheat cordial; serve hot.
Yield: about eighteen 2-ounce servings

Sausage-Stuffed Mushrooms

1 pound large fresh mushrooms
1/2 pound kielbasa, ground in food processor
1 cup finely chopped onion
1/2 cup butter
1 cup seasoned bread crumbs
1/2 cup grated Parmesan cheese
Garnish: fresh flat Italian parsley

Wipe mushrooms with a damp paper towel. Remove stems and finely chop. Sauté mushrooms stems, sausage, and onion in butter 10 minutes or until onion is tender. Remove from heat and stir in bread crumbs; fill each mushroom top with sausage mixture. Sprinkle with Parmesan cheese. Place on a greased baking pan; bake at 425° for 15 minutes or until filling is heated through. Garnish, if desired. Serve warm.
Yield: about 12 appetizers
Contributed by E. Knowles

White Chocolate-Peppermint Punch

Shown on page 115

1 container (half-gallon) vanilla ice cream, softened
3/4 cup crushed peppermint candies, divided
1 quart milk
6 ounces white baking chocolate, chopped
1 teaspoon vanilla extract
1 cup whipping cream
2 tablespoons confectioners sugar
1 bottle (1-liter) club soda
2 ounces white baking chocolate, shaved

Stir together ice cream and 1/2 cup crushed peppermint candies. Pour into an airtight container and freeze.

In a saucepan over medium-low heat, stir milk and chopped white chocolate until chocolate melts. Remove from heat and stir in vanilla. Chill until ready to serve.

To serve, soften ice cream mixture; set aside. Beat whipping cream until stiff peaks form, gradually adding confectioners sugar; set aside. Mix ice cream mixture, milk mixture, and club soda in punch bowl. Place dollops of sweetened whipped cream on top and sprinkle with remaining 1/4 cup crushed candies and shaved white chocolate.
Yield: about twenty-three 6-ounce servings

Cheesy, Cheesy Cheddar Ring

Cheesy, Cheesy Cheddar Ring

- 4 cups shredded sharp Cheddar cheese
- 1 cup mayonnaise
- 1 bunch green onions, chopped
- 1/4 cup chopped pecans, toasted
- 1 garlic clove, minced
- 1/2 teaspoon hot sauce
  Garnish: pecan halves, chopped green onion tops, sliced strawberry
  Strawberry preserves and small toasts or crackers to serve

Combine Cheddar cheese, mayonnaise, onions, chopped pecans, garlic, and hot sauce. Press mixture into a greased 6-cup ring mold; chill until ready to serve.

Remove cheese ring from mold onto a serving plate. Garnish sides with pecan halves and sprinkle top with green onions, if desired.

To serve, spoon strawberry preserves into center of ring. Garnish with sliced strawberry, if desired. Serve with small toasts or crackers.

Yield: 20 to 25 appetizer servings

Turkey Nachos

Turkey Nachos

- 1 can (16 ounces) refried beans
- 1 teaspoon chili powder
- 1 teaspoon ground cumin
- 2 tablespoons vegetable oil
- 1 pound deli turkey breast, diced (about 3$^1/_2$ cups)
- $^1/_2$ cup chopped onion
- 1 can (4 ounces) chopped mild green chilies
- 2 tablespoons chopped fresh cilantro leaves
- 1 teaspoon salt
- $^1/_2$ teaspoon pepper
- 1 cup finely chopped tomato
- 1 bag (10$^1/_2$ ounces) round tortilla chips
- 2 cups (8 ounces) shredded Monterey Jack cheese

In a small saucepan, combine beans, chili powder, and cumin. Cook, stirring occasionally, over medium-low heat until heated through. Remove from heat and cover.

In a large skillet, heat oil over medium heat. Add turkey, onion, chilies, cilantro, salt, and pepper. Cook, stirring occasionally, until onion is tender. Remove from heat and stir in tomato.

Spread about 1 teaspoon bean mixture on each tortilla chip; place in a single layer on a greased baking sheet. Spoon about 1 tablespoon turkey mixture over bean mixture. Sprinkle cheese evenly over turkey mixture. Bake at 425° for 5 to 7 minutes or until cheese melts. Serve warm.

Yield: about 4$^1/_2$ dozen nachos

Fresh Salsa Verde

- 1 pound fresh tomatillos, hulled and finely chopped
- $^3/_4$ cup finely chopped onion
- $^1/_4$ cup water
- $^1/_2$ teaspoon salt
- 1 avocado, seeded, peeled, and chopped
- $^1/_4$ cup chopped fresh cilantro
- 2 tablespoons freshly squeezed lime juice
- 2 to 3 garlic cloves, minced
- 1 small fresh jalapeño pepper, seeded and chopped
- $^1/_4$ teaspoon black pepper
  Tortilla chips to serve

In a medium saucepan over medium heat, combine tomatillos, onion, water, and salt. Cover and cook about 15 minutes or until tomatillos are tender; drain. In a medium bowl, combine tomatillo mixture and remaining ingredients except tortilla chips.

Cover and chill 2 hours to let flavors blend. Serve with tortilla chips.

Yield: about 2 cups salsa

Crispy Coconut Shrimp

Shrimp

- 1 cup flat beer
- 1 cup self-rising flour
- 2 cups sweetened coconut flakes, divided
- 2 tablespoons sugar
- 1/2 teaspoon salt
- 1 package (16 ounces) frozen uncooked jumbo shrimp, thawed
  Paprika
  Vegetable oil for frying

Dipping Sauce

- 1 jar (18 ounces) apricot-pineapple preserves
- 4 teaspoons spicy brown mustard
- 1 tablespoon prepared horseradish
- 1/4 teaspoon salt

For shrimp, beat beer, flour, 1/2 cup coconut, sugar, and salt together until well blended. Cover and refrigerate for at least 1 hour.

Leaving shells on tails, peel and devein shrimp. Pat shrimp dry with paper towels and sprinkle with paprika. Dip shrimp into batter and into remaining 1 1/2 cups coconut. Fry shrimp in hot oil 2 to 3 minutes or until lightly brown, turning once during cooking. Drain on paper towels and serve warm with dipping sauce.

For dipping sauce, combine all ingredients and refrigerate until ready to serve.

Yield: 16 to 20 shrimp and 1 3/4 cups dipping sauce

Contributed by Ron Werle

Fresh Salsa Verde

Crispy Coconut Shrimp

Cosmos for a Group

Cranberry Cheese Ball

Cranberry Cheese Ball

  1 package (8 ounces) cream
       cheese, softened
  1 container (8 ounces) sour
       cream
 3/4 cup sweetened, dried
       cranberries
 1/2 cup chopped green
       onions
1 1/2 cups chopped pecans,
       toasted and divided
 1/2 teaspoon curry powder
 1/4 teaspoon salt
       Garnish: coarsely chopped
         pecans, chopped green
         onion tops
       Crackers to serve

Mix cream cheese, sour cream, dried cranberries, onions, 1/2 cup pecans, curry powder, and salt. Place mixture on large piece of plastic wrap. Using plastic wrap, shape mixture into a ball; refrigerate until well chilled.

Roll cheese ball in remaining 1 cup pecans and garnish, if desired. Serve with crackers.

Yield: one cheese ball

Cosmos for a Group

2½ cups sweet and sour mix
1¼ cups vodka
5 ounces orange liqueur
1¼ cups cranberry juice
Crushed ice
Garnish: lemon zest strips

Mix all ingredients in a pitcher. Serve over crushed ice. Garnish, if desired.
Yield: about ten 4.5-ounce servings
Contributed by Ron Werle

Cranberry Sangria
Shown on page 130

1 bottle (750 ml) Burgundy
3 cups cranberry juice cocktail
¼ cup brandy
¼ cup sugar
1 can (8 ounces) pineapple chunks, drained
Garnish: maraschino cherries, orange slices, wooden skewers

Combine Burgundy, cranberry juice, brandy, and sugar in a 2-quart container. Stir until sugar dissolves. Cover and refrigerate until ready to serve.

To serve, add ice and pour sangria into glasses. Garnish, if desired.
Yield: about eight 6-ounce servings

Mulled Cranberry Port
Shown on page 118

4 cups cranberry juice cocktail
1 can (6 ounces) frozen orange juice concentrate
½ cup sugar
1 tablespoon whole cloves
½ teaspoon whole allspice
1 cinnamon stick
2 medium oranges, sliced
1 bottle (750 ml) tawny or ruby port wine
Cinnamon sticks and orange slices to serve

Combine cranberry juice cocktail, orange juice concentrate, and sugar in a Dutch oven over medium-high heat. Place cloves and allspice in a coffee filter tied with kitchen string and add to juice mixture. Add 1 cinnamon stick and 2 orange slices. Bring to a boil. Reduce heat to low; add wine and stir until mixture is heated through. Serve hot with additional cinnamon sticks and orange slices.
Yield: about ten 6-ounce servings

Hot Cranberry Punch

5 cups unsweetened pineapple juice
5 cups cranberry juice cocktail
1 cup firmly packed brown sugar
2 cans (16 ounces each) cranberry sauce
1½ cups water
1 teaspoon whole cloves
2 cinnamon sticks
½ cup butter

In a stockpot, combine juices, brown sugar, cranberry sauce, and water. Place the whole cloves and cinnamon sticks in a coffee filter tied with kitchen string and add to juice mixture. Bring mixture to a slow boil; reduce heat and simmer for 1 hour. Stir in butter just before serving or float a small piece of butter in each cup.
Yield: about twenty-seven 4-ounce servings

Wassail Punch

    4 cups apple cider
    1 cup applejack brandy
       (optional)
    1/4 cup lemon juice
    1/4 cup firmly packed brown
       sugar
    1/2 teaspoon whole allspice
    1/2 teaspoon whole cloves
    1/8 teaspoon ground nutmeg
       Garnish: thin apple slices

Combine all ingredients, except garnish, in a large saucepan. Cook over medium heat until heated through. Remove whole spices before serving. Garnish, if desired.
Yield: seven 6-ounce servings

Yogurt Smoothie

    1 ripe banana, peeled and
       cut into pieces
    1 carton (8 ounce) vanilla
       low-fat yogurt
    1 cup orange juice

Combine all ingredients in a blender. Process 2 minutes or until smooth.
Yield: 2 1/2 cups smoothie

Citrus Punch

    1 can (12 ounces) frozen
       lemonade concentrate,
       thawed
    1 can (12 ounces) frozen
       limeade concentrate,
       thawed
    1 can (12 ounces)
       frozen orange juice
       concentrate, thawed
    2 quarts water
    1 bottle (2 liters) ginger ale
    1 quart orange sherbet

Combine juice concentrates and water; stir until well blended. Chill until ready to serve.

To serve, pour juice mixture into a large container or punch bowl; stir in ginger ale and top with scoops of sherbet.
Yield: about 35 servings

Wassail Punch

Orange Cream

Honey-of-a-Punch

- 5 cups unsweetened pineapple juice
- 5 cups cranberry juice cocktail
- 2 cups water
- 1 cup honey
- 2 tablespoons whole allspice
- 4 two-inch cinnamon sticks

Place first 4 ingredients in a large Dutch oven. Place allspice and cinnamon sticks in a coffee filter tied with kitchen string and add spices to juice mixture. Simmer over medium-low heat 1 hour. Serve hot. (Punch may also be prepared by placing first 4 ingredients in a large electric percolator. Stir until well blended. Place allspice and cinnamon sticks in percolator basket. Perk through complete cycle.)
Yield: about seventeen 6-ounce servings

Orange Cream

- 4 cups orange juice
- 3 cinnamon sticks
- 1 tablespoon vanilla extract
- 1 container (pint) vanilla ice cream
  Miniature marshmallows to serve

In a large saucepan, combine orange juice, cinnamon sticks, and vanilla over medium-high heat. Bring mixture to a boil and reduce to low heat. Simmer 10 minutes. Remove cinnamon sticks. Stir in ice cream. Cook over low heat, stirring constantly, until heated through. Do not allow mixture to boil. Serve with miniature marshmallows.
Yield: 4 to 6 servings

Praline Coffee
Shown on page 121

- 3 cups hot brewed coffee
- 3/4 cup firmly packed light brown sugar
- 3/4 cup half-and-half
- 3/4 cup praline liqueur
  Garnish: sweetened whipped cream, toffee bits

Cook coffee, brown sugar, and half-and-half in a large saucepan over medium heat, stirring constantly, until heated through (do not boil). Stir in liqueur. Garnish coffee with dollops of sweetened whipped cream sprinkled with toffee bits.
Yield: 5 cups coffee

appetizers & beverages ❊ *99*

Strawberry Salad Supreme

- 2 packages (3 ounces each) strawberry gelatin
- 2 cups boiling water
- 1 can (20 ounces) crushed pineapple, drained and juice reserved
- 1 package (16 ounces) frozen sweetened strawberries
- 3 bananas, sliced
- 1 envelope (1.4 ounces) whipped topping mix and ingredients to prepare
- 1 package (8 ounces) cream cheese, softened
- 3/4 cup sugar
- 2 eggs, beaten
- 2 tablespoons all-purpose flour
- 1 tablespoon lemon juice
- 1 cup chopped pecans

Place gelatin in a large bowl; add boiling water and stir until gelatin dissolves. Stir in pineapple, strawberries (including juice) and bananas. Pour into a 9" x 13" pan; chill until firm.

Prepare whipped topping according to package directions. Blend in cream cheese. Spread on congealed gelatin; cover and chill.

Add enough water to reserved pineapple juice to make 1 cup. Combine pineapple juice mixture, sugar, eggs, flour, and lemon juice in a saucepan over low heat. Cook, stirring constantly, until mixture thickens; chill. Spread over cream cheese layer and sprinkle with pecans.

Yield: 12 to 14 servings

Contributed by Linda Sunwall

Rainbow Fruit Salad

- 1 can (14 ounces) sweetened condensed milk
- 1/4 cup frozen lemonade concentrate, thawed
- 1 can (16 ounces) mandarin oranges, drained
- 1 can (20 ounces) pineapple chunks, drained
- 2 kiwifruit, peeled and sliced
- 1 pint strawberries, capped and sliced

In a large bowl, beat condensed milk and lemonade using medium speed of an electric mixer. Stir in remaining ingredients by hand until fruit is well coated. Store in an airtight container in refrigerator.

Yield: about 10 servings

Curried Chicken Salad Sandwiches
(recipe on page 104)

Strawberry Salad Supreme

Eggnog Tarts
(recipe on page 112)

Sweet Potato-Squash Soup

This soup can be stored in the refrigerator for three days or frozen for three months.

- 1 teaspoon ground cardamom
- 1 teaspoon ground turmeric
- 1 teaspoon ground cinnamon
- 1/2 teaspoon ground cumin
- 1 tablespoon butter
- 1 tablespoon olive oil
- 2 cups chopped onion
- 8 cups peeled and diced fresh sweet potatoes
- 1 butternut squash (about 1 1/2 pounds), peeled and diced
- 2 carrots, peeled and sliced
- 2 1/2 quarts canned chicken broth
  Salt and pepper

Combine cardamom, turmeric, cinnamon, and cumin in a small bowl; set aside. In a large stockpot, heat butter and oil over medium heat. Add onion; cook, stirring occasionally, until tender. Stir in spices, sweet potatoes, squash, and carrots. Add chicken broth to mixture and bring to a simmer; cook over low heat, partially covered, until vegetables are tender. Add salt and pepper to taste. Remove from heat.

Process soup in a blender until smooth, working in batches. Return puréed mixture to stockpot and heat until warm.
Yield: 10 servings

Pumpkin Soup

Pumpkin Soup may be served in a hollowed-out pumpkin.

- 1 pound cooked smoked sausage (such as kielbasa), cut into 1/2-inch slices
- 1 tablespoon butter or margarine
- 1 tablespoon vegetable oil
- 1/4 cup all-purpose flour
- 1 pound stew meat, cut into 1-inch cubes
- 1 1/2 cups chopped onion
- 2/3 cup chopped celery
- 5 cups water
- 1 1/2 cups sliced carrots
- 1/2 teaspoon dried thyme
- 1 1/2 teaspoons salt
- 1/4 teaspoon pepper
- 1 bay leaf
- 2 1/2 cups 1/2-inch cubes of peeled pumpkin or winter squash

Place sausage in a large saucepan and add enough water to cover sausage. Bring to a boil and cook 3 minutes; drain and set aside.

In a Dutch oven, heat butter and oil over medium heat. Sprinkle flour over stew meat. Add stew meat to butter mixture and cook, stirring occasionally, until meat browns. Add onion and celery; cook until tender. Add sausage and next 6 ingredients; stir until well blended. Bring to a boil; reduce heat to low, cover, and simmer about 1 hour. Add pumpkin or winter squash and cook about 30 minutes or until tender. Remove bay leaf. Serve hot.
Yield: about 10 servings

Gougere

- 1/2 cup butter or margarine
- 1 1/4 cups all-purpose flour
- 4 eggs
- 3 cups shredded sharp Cheddar cheese
- 1 cup shredded Swiss cheese
- 1/2 teaspoon salt
- 1/4 teaspoon black pepper
- 1 garlic clove, minced
- 2 jalapeño peppers, chopped
- 1/4 cup chopped onion
- 1/8 teaspoon cayenne pepper

In a medium saucepan, melt butter over medium heat. Add flour and stir until mixture forms a ball. Remove from heat and continue stirring until mixture cools. Beat in eggs, one at a time, stirring until mixture is slightly glossy and smooth. Stir in remaining ingredients. Pour batter into a greased 10-inch iron skillet. Bake at 375° for 40 to 45 minutes or until golden brown.
Yield: about 16 servings

Oatmeal-Rye Rolls

Shown on page 109

- 2 cups water
- 1 cup old-fashioned rolled oats
- 3 cups all-purpose flour
- 2 cups whole-wheat flour
- 1 cup rye flour
- 1/2 cup nonfat dry milk
- 2 1/2 teaspoons salt
- 2 packages rapid-rising dry yeast
- 1/3 cup warm water
- 1/2 cup honey
- 1/4 cup vegetable oil
  Vegetable cooking spray

In a medium saucepan, bring 2 cups water to a boil over high heat. Remove from heat; stir in oats. Cool to room temperature.

In a large bowl, sift together flours, dry milk, and salt. In a small bowl, dissolve yeast in 1/3 cup warm water. Add oats mixture, yeast mixture, honey, and oil to dry ingredients. Stir until a soft dough forms. Turn onto a lightly floured surface and knead until dough becomes smooth and elastic. Place in a large bowl sprayed with cooking spray, turning once to coat top of dough. Cover and let rise in a warm place (80° to 85°) 1 hour or until doubled in size. Turn dough onto a lightly floured surface and punch down. Shape dough into 2" balls and place 2" apart on a greased baking sheet. Spray tops of rolls with cooking spray, cover, and let rise in a warm place 1 hour or until doubled in size.

Preheat oven to 350°. Bake 25 to 30 minutes or until golden brown. Serve warm or cool completely on a wire rack.

Yield: about 2 dozen rolls

Gougere

Pumpkin Soup

103

Top Sirloin Roast

- 1 top sirloin butt roast (5 pounds)
- 1/2 cup (3.4-ounce jar) steak seasoning
- 4 tablespoons dried rosemary
- 2 tablespoons coarsely ground black pepper
- 1 tablespoon kosher salt
- 1 heaping tablespoon dried basil
- 4 tablespoons olive oil, divided
- 4 garlic cloves
   Garnish: fresh rosemary sprigs, fresh cranberries

Remove roast from refrigerator one hour before baking.

Mix steak seasoning, rosemary, pepper, salt, basil, and 2 tablespoons olive oil. Cut four slits in bottom of roast and insert garlic. Rub roast with remaining 2 tablespoons oil and cover top and sides with seasoning mixture. Bake roast in a 325° oven for 15 minutes per pound or until internal temperature reaches 130° for medium-rare, 140° for medium, or 150° for well done. Remove from oven and cover with aluminum foil. Let roast stand for 20 minutes before slicing. Garnish, if desired.
Yield: 8 to 10 servings

Curried Chicken Salad Sandwiches
Shown on page 101

- 5 cups cubed cooked chicken breasts
- 1 cup mayonnaise
- 1/2 cup shredded Swiss cheese
- 2 tablespoons dried parsley
- 1 teaspoon dried mustard
- 1 teaspoon celery seed
- 1 teaspoon curry
- 1 teaspoon salt
- 1 cup chopped pecans, toasted
   Croissants
   Leafy lettuce

Stir together first 8 ingredients until well blended; stir in pecans. Serve on croissants with leafy lettuce.
Yield: 8 to 10 servings
Contributed by Jane Bell

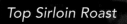
Top Sirloin Roast

Pork Tenderloin with Cranberry Sauce

- 1 pork tenderloin (about 2.30 pounds)
- 1 can (16 ounces) whole berry cranberry sauce
- 1/3 cup water
- 1 envelope (from a 2.0 ounce box) onion soup mix
  Spicy mustard to serve (optional)
  Small dinner rolls to serve
- 1 can (16 ounces) jellied cranberry sauce

Place tenderloin in a baking pan. Combine whole berry cranberry sauce, water, and soup mix; spread over tenderloin. Bake at 350° for 1 hour or until tenderloin reaches 160° internal temperature. Let stand 10 minutes before slicing.

Spread rolls with mustard before assembling, if desired. Serve pork on rolls with a thin slice of jellied cranberry sauce.

Yield: 20 to 25 sandwiches

Oyster Dressing

4 cups water
Giblets and neck from turkey
1 cup chopped onion
1 cup chopped celery
1/2 cup butter or margarine
3/4 cup sliced fresh mushrooms
7 cups crumbled corn bread
1/4 cup chopped fresh parsley
2 teaspoons poultry seasoning
2 teaspoons rubbed sage
1 teaspoon salt
2 containers (10 ounces each) fresh oysters, drained and chopped
2 eggs, beaten

Place water, giblets, and neck in a medium saucepan; bring to a boil over medium heat. Cover, reduce heat, and simmer 1 hour or until meat is tender. Reserve broth and chop meat.

In a medium skillet, sauté onion and celery in butter over medium heat. When vegetables are almost tender, add mushrooms; cook 2 minutes and remove from heat. In a large bowl, combine corn bread, parsley, poultry seasoning, sage, salt, meat, and vegetables. Stir in oysters, eggs, and 2 cups of giblet broth, adding additional broth as necessary, to moisten. Spoon into a greased 9" x 13" baking dish. Cover and bake at 350° for 45 minutes. Uncover and bake 15 to 20 minutes more or until lightly browned.
Yield: 12 to 14 servings

Broccoli-Almond Casserole

1 package (16 ounces) frozen chopped broccoli, cooked and drained
1/4 cup slivered almonds, toasted
2 tablespoons butter or margarine
2 tablespoons all-purpose flour
2 cups milk
3/4 cup shredded Cheddar cheese
1 teaspoon salt
1/4 teaspoon pepper
1/2 cup bread crumbs
2 tablespoons butter, melted
4 slices bacon, cooked and crumbled

Place broccoli in a greased 2-quart casserole dish. Sprinkle almonds over broccoli. For cheese sauce, melt 2 tablespoons butter in a saucepan. Whisk in flour; gradually whisk in milk until mixture is smooth. Continue cooking, whisking constantly, until mixture thickens. Stir in cheese, salt, and pepper; remove from heat. Pour in casserole. Mix bread crumbs with 2 tablespoons melted butter. Sprinkle bread crumbs and bacon pieces over top. Bake at 350° for 20 minutes or until bubbly.
Yield: 8 to 10 servings

Cheesy Tators

1 package (32 ounces) frozen cubed hash browns
2 cups shredded sharp Cheddar cheese
1 can (10 3/4 ounces) cream of chicken soup
1 cup sour cream
1 cup butter, melted and divided
1/2 cup chopped onion
1 teaspoon salt
1/2 teaspoon pepper
1 cup crushed corn flake cereal

Place potatoes in a greased 9" x 13" baking dish. Combine cheese, soup, sour cream, 1/2 cup melted butter, onion, salt, and pepper; pour over potatoes. Combine cereal and remaining 1/2 cup melted butter; spread over potato mixture. Bake at 350° for 35 to 45 minutes or until top is lightly browned.
Yield: 10 to 12 servings
Contributed by Jennifer Hutchings

24-Hour Wine & Cheese Bake

Italian Sausage Frittata

24-Hour Wine & Cheese Bake

You can substitute any cheese or meat you prefer. If you use bacon or sausage, it should be pre-cooked.

1	baguette (1 pound), day old
1½	cups shredded Swiss cheese
1	cup shredded Monterey Jack cheese
1	package (5 ounces) Canadian bacon, diced
1	bunch green onions, chopped
6	tablespoons butter, melted
16	eggs
3¼	cups whole milk
½	cup white wine
1	tablespoon Dijon mustard
¼	teaspoon black pepper
¼	teaspoon cayenne pepper
½	cup grated Parmesan cheese

Cut baguette into small bite-size cubes. Butter a 9"x13" baking dish. Place bread evenly on the bottom of the dish. Combine Swiss and Monterey Jack cheeses; sprinkle over bread. Top cheeses with Canadian bacon and green onions. Drizzle with melted butter. In a large bowl, whisk together eggs, milk, wine, mustard, and peppers. Add egg mixture to dish. Cover with aluminum foil and refrigerate overnight or for at least 4 to 6 hours.

Remove dish from refrigerator at least 30 minutes before baking. Place covered dish in a preheated 325° oven for 1 hour. Remove foil and sprinkle with Parmesan cheese; bake for another 10 to 15 minutes or until edges are lightly browned and center is set.
Yield: 12 servings

Deep-Dish Vegetable Pie

Crust

- 1 package dry yeast
- ²/₃ cup warm water
- 2 cups all-purpose flour, divided
- ¹/₂ cup finely crushed corn chips
- 1 tablespoon sugar
- 2 teaspoons finely chopped onion
- ³/₄ teaspoon salt
- 2 tablespoons vegetable oil

Filling

- 1 tablespoon vegetable oil
- 1 tablespoon butter or margarine
- 3 cups fresh broccoli flowerets
- 3 cups shredded cabbage
- 2 cups thinly sliced zucchini
- 1¹/₂ cups chopped onions
- 1¹/₂ cups thinly sliced carrots
- 1 teaspoon salt
- ¹/₂ teaspoon pepper
- ¹/₄ teaspoon garlic powder
- ¹/₄ teaspoon chili powder
- 1¹/₂ cups shredded sharp Cheddar cheese

For crust, dissolve yeast in water in a small bowl. In a medium bowl, combine 1 cup flour, corn chips, sugar, onion, and salt; stir until well blended. Add yeast mixture and oil to dry ingredients. Stir until smooth. Add remaining 1 cup flour; stir until well blended. On a lightly floured surface, use a floured rolling pin to roll out dough to a 13" diameter circle.

Press dough into bottom and 2" up sides of a well-greased 9" springform pan. Cover and let rise in a warm place (80° to 85°) 10 minutes. Prick bottom of crust with a fork. Bake at 375° for 25 to 30 minutes or until golden brown.

For filling, heat oil and butter in a large skillet over medium-high heat. Add next 9 ingredients. Stirring constantly, cook vegetables until just tender. Spoon vegetables over warm crust using a slotted spoon. Sprinkle cheese evenly over vegetables. Bake at 375° for 8 to 10 minutes or until cheese is bubbly. Cut into wedges and serve warm.

Yield: about 10 servings

Italian Sausage Frittata

You can also use leftover ham or turkey instead of the sausage.

- 1 small onion, sliced
- ³/₄ pound Italian sausage, cooked and crumbled
- 1 cup sliced fresh mushrooms, divided
- 1 small zucchini, thinly sliced
- 1 small red bell pepper, sliced into rings
- 12 eggs, beaten
- ¹/₃ cup freshly grated Parmesan cheese

In a greased 10" deep-dish pie plate, layer onion, sausage, ³/₄ cup mushrooms, zucchini, and red pepper. Pour eggs over vegetables; sprinkle cheese over eggs. Arrange remaining ¹/₄ cup mushrooms in center. Bake at 350° for 40 to 45 minutes or until edges are lightly browned. Cut into wedges and serve.

Yield: 6 to 8 servings

Deep-Dish Vegetable Pie

Oatmeal-Rye Rolls
(recipe on page 103)

Glazed Roasted Turkey with Horseradish Sauce

Glazed Turkey

1½ cups apple jelly
½ cup balsamic vinegar
1 tablespoon grated lemon zest
2 teaspoons salt
1½ teaspoons pepper
1 turkey (13 to 15 pounds)
 Salt and pepper
1 cup water

Horseradish Sauce

2 tablespoons butter or margarine
¾ cup minced onion
2 tablespoons all-purpose flour
½ cup chicken broth
¾ cup apple jelly
1 jar (5 ounces) cream-style prepared horseradish
½ teaspoon salt
⅛ teaspoon white pepper
½ cup whipping cream

For glazed turkey, combine jelly, vinegar, lemon zest, 2 teaspoons salt, and 1½ teaspoons pepper in a small saucepan. Stirring frequently, cook over medium heat until jelly melts. Remove glaze from heat.

Remove giblets and neck from turkey. Rinse turkey and pat dry. Salt and pepper inside of turkey. Tie ends of legs to tail with kitchen twine.

Place turkey, breast side up, in a large roasting pan. Insert meat thermometer into thickest part of thigh, making sure thermometer does not touch bone. Pour water into pan. Baste turkey with glaze. Loosely cover with aluminum foil. Basting with glaze every 30 minutes, bake at 350° for 3 to 3½ hours or until meat thermometer registers 180° and juices run clear when thickest part of thigh is pierced with a fork. Remove foil during last hour to allow turkey to brown. Transfer turkey to a serving platter and let stand 20 minutes before carving.

For horseradish sauce, melt butter in a heavy medium saucepan over medium heat. Add onion and sauté about 6 minutes or until onion is transparent. Stirring constantly, add flour and cook 3 minutes or until mixture is bubbly. Stir in chicken broth; continue to stir until thick and well blended. Stir in jelly, horseradish, salt, and white pepper; cook until jelly melts. Gradually stir in whipping cream and bring to a simmer. Serve warm sauce over turkey.
Yield: 15 to 18 servings

Potato Gratiné

2 large russet potatoes, peeled and cut into thin slices
1½ cups shredded Cheddar cheese
¾ cup whipping cream
¾ cup dry white wine
4 eggs
1 teaspoon salt
½ teaspoon ground white pepper
½ teaspoon garlic powder
 Garnish: chopped fresh parsley

Place potato slices in a large saucepan and cover with water. Bring to a boil and cook until potatoes are tender; drain.

Press aluminum foil around bottoms of 8 greased 4" tart pans with removable bottoms. Arrange potato slices in pans. Sprinkle cheese evenly over potatoes.

In a medium bowl, whisk cream, wine, eggs, salt, pepper, and garlic powder; pour evenly over potatoes. Place tart pans on a baking sheet. Bake at 350° for 25 to 30 minutes or until tops are golden and cheese is melted. To serve, remove sides and bottoms of pans. Garnish, if desired.
Yield: 8 servings

Potato Gratiné
Green Beans with Apples

Green Beans with Apples

  1 sweet onion, thinly sliced into rings
 ¼ cup butter
  1 package (16 ounces) frozen whole green
     beans
  1 sweet unpeeled red apple, thinly sliced
     Salt and pepper

Sauté onion in butter in a skillet until onion is transparent. Cook beans according to package directions until crisp tender; drain. Add beans and apple slices to skillet; stir until well coated with butter. Season with salt and pepper.

Yield: 6 servings
Contributed by Ron Werle

Sweets & Desserts

At Christmastime, you only want the best of the best. This big assortment of heavenly flavors and melt-in-your-mouth richness includes candy, cookies, pies, cakes, puddings, tarts, and cheesecakes. Pamper everyone with these astonishingly good recipes!

Apple Dumplings

- 2 Granny Smith apples, peeled and cored
- 1 can (8 ounces) refrigerated crescent rolls
- 1 cup orange juice
- 1 cup sugar
- 1/2 cup butter or margarine, melted
- 1 teaspoon ground cinnamon
- 1/2 cup chopped pecans
  Garnish: whipped cream and unpeeled Granny Smith apple slices

Cut each apple into 4 slices. Separate crescent roll dough into 8 pieces. Wrap each dough piece around one apple slice. Place in an 8" square pan. Combine orange juice, sugar, butter, and cinnamon; stir in pecans. Pour orange juice mixture over dough pieces. Bake at 375° for 20 minutes or until tops are lightly browned. Garnish, if desired.
Yield: 8 servings

Eggnog Tarts

Shown on page 101
The tart shells are found in the specialty cookie section.

- 1 package (3.12 ounces) vanilla pudding mix
- 1 envelope unflavored gelatin
- 1/8 teaspoon ground nutmeg
- 3 cups purchased eggnog
- 1/4 cup light rum (optional)
- 1/2 cup whipping cream, whipped
- 1 package (8.5-ounce package of 12) tart shells
  Garnish: ground nutmeg

Combine pudding mix, gelatin, and 1/8 teaspoon nutmeg in a saucepan; slowly stir in eggnog. Cook over medium heat, stirring constantly, until mixture boils; remove from heat. Stir in rum, if using. Chill 2 hours or until almost set.

Beat pudding mixture until fluffy; fold in whipped cream. Spoon into tart shells and refrigerate until ready to serve. Garnish, if desired.
Yield: 12 servings

Snickerdoodles

- 1 cup butter or margarine, softened
- 1 1/2 cups sugar, divided
- 2 eggs
- 1 teaspoon vanilla extract
- 2 1/2 cups all-purpose flour
- 1 1/2 teaspoons ground cinnamon, divided
- 1 teaspoon cream of tartar
- 1 teaspoon baking soda
- 1/4 teaspoon salt

In a large bowl, cream butter and 1 1/4 cups sugar until fluffy. Add eggs and vanilla; beat until smooth. In a medium bowl, combine flour, 1/2 teaspoon cinnamon, cream of tartar, baking soda, and salt. Add dry ingredients to creamed mixture; stir until a soft dough forms. In a small bowl, combine remaining 1/4 cup sugar and 1 teaspoon cinnamon. Shape dough into 1" balls and roll in sugar mixture. Place balls 2" apart on a lightly greased baking sheet. Bake at 375° for 6 to 8 minutes or until bottoms are lightly browned. Transfer cookies to a wire rack to cool. Store in an airtight container.
Yield: about 7 dozen cookies

Apple Dumplings

Hot Lemon Soufflé

Hot Lemon Soufflé

Butter and sugar
3 eggs, separated
3/4 cup sugar, divided
1 cup milk
4 tablespoons butter, melted
3 tablespoons all-purpose flour
1/4 cup lemon juice
1 tablespoon grated lemon zest
1/4 teaspoon cream of tartar
2 cups whipping cream, whipped
Garnish: lemon zest strips

Place rack in lower third of oven and preheat to 375°. Butter a 1-quart soufflé dish and sprinkle with sugar. Beat egg yolks with 1/2 cup of sugar until light in color. Beat in milk, butter, and flour. Stir in lemon juice and zest. In a separate bowl, beat egg whites until foamy. Add remaining 1/4 cup sugar and cream of tartar; beat until stiff and gently fold into egg yolk mixture. Pour into prepared dish. Set dish in a roasting pan in oven and add hot water to pan to come 1/3 up sides of dish. Bake for 30 to 35 minutes or until a wooden skewer inserted about 2" from the edge comes out with a few crumbs and top is golden brown. Top with whipped cream and garnish, if desired. Serve immediately.
Yield: 6 to 8 servings

Peanut Butter Divinity

2 cups sugar
1/2 cup light corn syrup
1/2 cup water
1/8 teaspoon salt
2 egg whites
1 teaspoon vanilla extract
1 cup crunchy peanut butter

Butter sides of a large heavy saucepan. Combine first 4 ingredients in pan and cook over medium-low heat, stirring constantly until sugar dissolves. Syrup will become clear. Using a pastry brush dipped in hot water, wash down any sugar crystals on sides of pan. Attach a candy thermometer to pan, making sure thermometer does not touch bottom of pan. Increase heat to medium and bring to a boil. Do not stir while syrup is boiling.

While syrup is boiling, use highest speed of an electric mixer to beat egg whites in a large bowl until stiff.

Continue to cook syrup until it reaches firm ball stage (approximately 242° to 248°). Test about 1/2 teaspoon syrup in ice water. Syrup will form a firm ball in ice water but will flatten if pressed when removed from water. While beating egg whites at low speed, slowly pour syrup into egg whites. Add vanilla and increase speed of mixer to high. Continue to beat until candy is no longer glossy. Fold in peanut butter. Pour into a buttered 8" square baking dish. Allow to harden. Cut into 1" squares. Store in an airtight container in refrigerator.
Yield: about 5 dozen candies

Snazzy Peach Cake

- 1 can (15.25 ounces) sliced peaches
- 1 cup sugar
- $1/2$ cup peach schnapps or orange juice
- $1/4$ cup orange juice
- 1 package (18.25 ounces) yellow cake mix
- 1 package (3.0 ounces) vanilla instant pudding mix
- 4 eggs
- $2/3$ cup vegetable oil
- 1 cup chopped pecans
- $1 3/4$ cups confectioners sugar
- 5 tablespoons whipping cream
- 1 teaspoon vanilla extract

In a glass bowl, combine undrained peaches, sugar, peach schnapps, and $1/4$ cup orange juice. Cover and let stand for 24 hours at room temperature.

Drain peach slices, reserving liquid; chop peaches. Beat cake mix, pudding mix, eggs, oil, and $1/3$ cup of reserved peach liquid for 2 minutes. Stir in pecans and chopped peaches. Pour into a greased and floured fluted tube pan. Bake at 350°for 40 to 45 minutes or until a toothpick inserted in center comes out clean. Cool in pan on a wire rack for 10 minutes. Remove from pan and cool completely on a wire rack.

In a small bowl, combine confectioners sugar, whipping cream, and vanilla. Drizzle over cake.

Yield: 12 to 16 servings
Contributed by Valerie Way

Wassail Punch
(recipe on page 98)

Snazzy Peach Cake

White Chocolate Peppermint Punch
(recipe on page 92)

Bourbon Balls

Bourbon Balls

2 1/2 cups pecans, finely chopped and divided
2 1/2 cups finely crushed vanilla wafer cookies
1 cup confectioners sugar
3 tablespoons bourbon
3 tablespoons light corn syrup
   Butter, softened
3/4 cup semisweet chocolate chips
1 tablespoon shortening

Combine 1 1/2 cups pecans, crushed cookies, confectioners sugar, bourbon, and corn syrup. Coat finger tips with softened butter and shape mixture into 1" diameter balls. Roll half of the balls in remaining 1 cup chopped pecans. Melt chocolate chips and shortening in top of a double boiler over simmering water. Dip remaining balls into chocolate. Place on waxed paper to harden.
Yield: about 4 dozen balls

Peanut Butter-Fudge Cookies

1 cup chunky peanut butter
2 tablespoons vegetable oil
2 eggs
1 package (21.5 ounces) fudge brownie mix
1/2 cup water
1 package (6 ounces) semisweet chocolate chips
1 cup chopped unsalted peanuts

In a large bowl, beat peanut butter, oil, and eggs. Add brownie mix and water; stir until moistened. Stir in chocolate chips. Drop tablespoonfuls of dough onto an ungreased baking sheet. Place 1/2 teaspoon peanuts on each cookie. Bake at 350° for 12 to 14 minutes or until fingertip leaves a slight indentation when center of cookie is touched. Transfer to a wire rack to cool completely. Store in an airtight container.
Yield: about 5 dozen cookies

Coconut Cream Cake

Cake

- 1 cup butter or margarine, softened
- 2 cups sugar
- 5 eggs
- 1 teaspoon vanilla extract
- 2 cups all-purpose flour
- 1 teaspoon baking soda
- $1/2$ teaspoon salt
- 1 cup buttermilk
- 2 cups sweetened shredded coconut
- 1 cup finely chopped pecans

Frosting

- 2 cups whipping cream
- $1/3$ cup sugar
- $1/3$ cup sour cream
- 3 cups sweetened shredded coconut, divided

For cake, cream butter and sugar in a large bowl until fluffy. Add eggs, 1 at a time, beating well after each addition. Stir in vanilla. In another large bowl, sift together next 3 ingredients. Stir dry ingredients and buttermilk alternately into creamed mixture. Fold in coconut and pecans. Pour batter into 3 greased and floured 9" round cake pans. Bake at 350° for 30 to 35 minutes or until a toothpick inserted in center comes out clean. Cool in pans 10 minutes; turn onto wire racks to cool completely.

For frosting, whip cream in a chilled large bowl until soft peaks form. Gradually adding sugar, beat until stiff peaks form. Fold in sour cream and 2 cups coconut. Spread about $1/3$ cup frosting between layers of cake. Spread remaining frosting on sides and top of cake. Sprinkle remaining 1 cup coconut on top and sides of cake.

Yield: about 20 servings

Peanut Butter-Fudge Cookies

Coconut Cream Cake

117

Gingerbread Brownies
Triple Chip Cookies

Spicy Cranberry-Nut Cake

Mulled Cranberry Port
(recipe on page 97)

Gingerbread Brownies

Brownies

- ¹/₂ cup butter or margarine, softened
- 1 cup granulated sugar
- 2 eggs
- 1 package (6 ounces) semisweet chocolate chips, melted
- ³/₄ cup hot water
- ³/₄ cup molasses
- 2¹/₂ cups all-purpose flour
- 2 teaspoons ground ginger
- 2 teaspoons baking soda
- ¹/₂ teaspoon salt
- 1 cup finely chopped walnuts

Icing

- 1 cup confectioners sugar, sifted
- 4 tablespoons milk

For brownies, cream butter and sugar until fluffy in a large bowl. Add eggs; beat until smooth. Add next 3 ingredients; stir until well blended. In a medium bowl, sift together next 4 ingredients. Add dry ingredients to creamed mixture; stir until well blended. Fold in walnuts. Pour batter into a greased 11" x 15" jellyroll pan. Bake at 350° for 30 to 35 minutes or until a toothpick inserted in center comes out clean. Cool completely on a wire rack.

For icing, stir sugar and milk together in a medium bowl until smooth. Ice brownies. Allow icing to harden. Cut into 2" squares. Store in an airtight container.

Yield: about 3 dozen brownies

Triple Chip Cookies

- 1/2 cup butter or margarine, softened
- 1/4 cup granulated sugar
- 1/4 cup firmly packed brown sugar
- 1 egg
- 1/2 teaspoon vanilla extract
- 1 1/4 cups all-purpose flour
- 1/2 teaspoon baking soda
- 1/4 teaspoon salt
- 1/2 cup plain granola cereal (without fruit and nuts)
- 1/3 cup semisweet chocolate chips
- 1/3 cup milk chocolate chips
- 1/3 cup white chocolate chips

In a large bowl, cream butter and sugars until fluffy. Add egg and vanilla; beat until smooth. In a small bowl, sift together next 3 ingredients. Stir in cereal. Add dry ingredients to creamed mixture; stir until a soft dough forms. Fold in chips. Drop by heaping teaspoonfuls 2" apart onto a greased baking sheet. Bake at 375° for 8 to 10 minutes or until edges are brown. Transfer to a wire rack to cool completely. Store in an airtight container.

Yield: about 3 1/2 dozen cookies

Spicy Cranberry-Nut Cake

Cake

- 8 eggs
- 1 tablespoon vanilla extract
- 2 cups sugar
- 1 cup all-purpose flour
- 4 teaspoons baking powder
- 1 teaspoon ground cinnamon
- 5 cups chopped pecans

Filling

- 1 can (8 1/4 ounces) crushed pineapple in heavy syrup
- 3 tablespoons cornstarch
- 1 can (16 ounces) whole berry cranberry sauce
  Red liquid food coloring

Icing

- 1 1/2 cups whipping cream
- 2 tablespoons confectioners sugar
- 1/4 teaspoon ground cinnamon
- 1/8 teaspoon ground mace

For cake, grease three 9" cake pans and line bottoms with waxed paper. In a large bowl, beat eggs and vanilla 5 minutes at high speed of an electric mixer. In a small bowl, combine sugar, flour, baking powder, and cinnamon. Reduce mixer to medium speed and add dry ingredients to egg mixture; beat 5 minutes. Reduce speed to low and stir in pecans. Pour batter into prepared pans. Bake at 350° for 25 to 30 minutes or until a toothpick inserted in center of cake comes out clean. Cool in pans on wire racks 5 minutes. Transfer cakes to wire racks to cool completely.

For filling, reserving 1/4 cup syrup, drain pineapple; combine syrup with cornstarch in a heavy medium saucepan. Add drained pineapple and cranberry sauce. Stirring constantly, cook over medium-high heat until mixture comes to a boil and thickens; reduce heat to medium and boil 2 minutes. Add 5 drops food coloring. Transfer filling to a covered container and chill 2 hours. Spread filling between layers and on top of cake.

For icing, place a small bowl and beaters from electric mixer in freezer to chill. In chilled bowl, beat icing ingredients until stiff peaks form. Ice sides of cake. Transfer remaining icing to a pastry bag fitted with a medium open star tip; pipe shell borders. Store in refrigerator until ready to serve.

Yield: about 12 servings

Cherry-Almond Fudge

Cherry-Almond Fudge

- 1/4 cup butter
- 2 1/2 cups confectioners sugar
- 2/3 cup milk
- 12 ounces white chocolate baking squares, coarsely chopped
- 3/4 cup chopped dried tart red cherries
- 3/4 cup sliced almonds, toasted
- 1/2 teaspoon almond extract (optional)
- 1 tube (4 1/4 ounces) pink decorating icing (optional)

Line an 8" x 8" x 2" baking pan with foil, extending foil over the edges of the pan; butter foil. Butter the sides of a heavy 2-quart saucepan. Combine confectioners sugar, milk, and 1/4 cup butter. Cook and stir over medium-high heat until mixture boils and sugar dissolves. Reduce heat to medium low. Boil gently, without stirring for 5 minutes. Reduce heat to low. Add white chocolate and stir until chocolate melts and mixture is smooth and creamy. Remove from heat; stir in cherries and almonds. Add almond extract, if desired. Immediately spread fudge in prepared pan. Cover and chill 6 hours or until firm. Use foil to lift fudge from pan.

Cut fudge into 1" x 2" pieces or desired size. If desired, use icing to decorate each piece. Fudge can be stored in an airtight container in refrigerator for up to one week.
Yield: about 2 pounds fudge

Madeleines

- 2 eggs
- 1/8 teaspoon salt
- 1/2 cup sugar
- 1/2 cup all-purpose flour
- 1/2 cup butter, melted and cooled
- Grand Marnier liqueur

In a large mixing bowl, combine eggs and salt. Gradually beat in sugar until mixture is thick and lightens in color (about 5 minutes). Fold flour into egg mixture a few tablespoons at a time. Fold in butter a few tablespoons at a time. Spoon 1 tablespoon of batter into each shell of a greased and floured Madeleine pan. Bake at 400° for 8 to 10 minutes or until a cake springs back when lightly touched. Immediately remove from molds and cool on wire racks. Sprinkle Madeleines with liqueur.
Yield: about 18 cakes

Apricot Turnovers

Pastry

- 1 package (8 ounces) cream cheese, softened
- 1 cup butter, softened
- 2 1/2 cups all-purpose flour
- 1/2 teaspoon salt

Filling

- 1 package (7 ounces) chopped dried apricots
- 2 tablespoons apricot preserves
- Confectioners sugar

For pastry, combine all ingredients in a medium bowl. Mix together well, using your hands; shape into a ball. Wrap in plastic wrap and chill at least 2 hours or overnight.

On a lightly floured surface, use a floured rolling pin to roll out dough to 1/8" thickness. Cut into 3" squares. For filling, mix apricots and preserves together. Spoon about 1/2 teaspoon filling into the center of each square. Fold dough in half diagonally over filling to form a triangle; lightly press edges together. Cut 3 slits in tops. Place on an ungreased baking sheet and bake at 350° for 10 to 14 minutes or until bottoms are lightly browned. Place on wire racks with waxed paper underneath and sprinkle with confectioners sugar.

Yield: about 3 dozen turnovers

Contributed by Jeanne Gartman from her grandmother Margaret Horvath

Apricot Turnovers

Praline Coffee
(recipe on page 99)

Mexican Bizcochitos

1 cup butter or margarine, softened
1 cup sugar, divided
1 egg yolk
1 tablespoon milk
2½ cups all-purpose flour
4½ teaspoons ground cinnamon, divided
2 teaspoons anise seed
½ cup white wine

In a large bowl, cream butter, ½ cup sugar, egg yolk, and milk. In another bowl, combine flour, 1½ teaspoons cinnamon, and anise seed. Add flour mixture to creamed mixture, stirring until combined. Stir in wine. Wrap dough in plastic wrap and chill at least 2 hours.

On a lightly floured surface, use a floured rolling pin to roll out dough to ⅛" thickness. Cut into desired shapes using 2" cookie cutters. Transfer cookies to lightly greased baking sheets and bake at 350° for 10 to 12 minutes or until edges are very lightly browned.

In a small bowl, combine remaining ½ cup sugar and remaining 3 teaspoons of cinnamon. Sprinkle warm cookies with sugar mixture. Store in an airtight container.
Yield: about 8 dozen cookies

Gingerbread Trees

This will make 3 trees.
Gingerbread

1 cup butter, softened
1 cup firmly packed brown sugar
1 cup molasses
2 eggs
6 cups all-purpose flour
1 tablespoon ground cinnamon
1 tablespoon ground ginger
1 teaspoon baking soda
1 teaspoon ground cloves
1 teaspoon ground allspice
1 teaspoon salt
½ teaspoon baking powder

Royal Icing

4 tablespoons meringue powder
6 cups confectioners sugar
9 tablespoons warm water
  Pastry bags with #5 and #12 decorating tips
  Pearlized sugar pearls

For gingerbread, beat butter and brown sugar until fluffy in a large bowl. Beat in molasses and eggs. Combine remaining ingredients in another large bowl. Stir dry ingredients into creamed mixture. Divide dough into 3 balls and wrap in plastic wrap; chill 1 hour.

Working with 1 ball of dough at a time, roll out dough on a lightly floured surface to ¼" thickness. Use pattern (page 158) and a small sharp knife to cut out 4 tree pieces for each tree. Transfer to ungreased or parchment-covered baking sheets. (Reuse excess dough.) Bake at 350° for 8 to 10 minutes or until firm to the touch. Cool on baking sheet; transfer to wire racks to cool completely.

For icing, beat meringue powder, confectioners sugar, and water in a medium bowl at high speed with an electric mixer 7 to 10 minutes or until stiff. Spoon into pastry bags fitted with suggested decorating tips (refill bag as necessary). Keep icing tightly covered when not using to prevent drying.

Assembling the Tree

(**Note:** Use icing to decorate and as "glue" to adhere the tree pieces together.) For each tree, you will need 4 tree pieces.
1. On waxed paper, place 2 tree pieces together with straight edges about ⅛" apart. Use #12 tip and pipe icing along straight edges to "glue" pieces together; allow to dry.
2. Stand the 2 tree pieces up and use cans to prop in place. Pipe icing along straight edge of third tree piece and adhere to iced area of first two pieces; prop in place. Repeat with fourth tree piece. Let icing harden. Remove cans.
3. Use #5 tip and pipe icing on sides and edges of trees for decorations, pressing pearls into wet icing. Allow to harden.

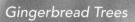
Gingerbread Trees

Irish Cream Fudge

Shown on page 89

- 2 packages (12 ounces) milk chocolate chips
- 1 package (12 ounces) semisweet chocolate chips
- 2 cups chopped pecans
- 1 jar (13 ounces) marshmallow creme
- 2/3 cup Irish cream liqueur
- 2 teaspoons vanilla extract
- 4 1/2 cups sugar
- 1 can (12 ounces) evaporated milk
- 1 cup butter

Combine chocolate chips, pecans, marshmallow creme, liqueur, and vanilla in a large bowl; set aside

Combine sugar, evaporated milk, and butter in a saucepan. Stirring constantly, bring to a boil; reduce heat to a simmer and cook 11 minutes, continuing to stir constantly. Pour mixture over ingredients in bowl and stir until chocolate chips are melted. Pour into a greased aluminum foil-lined 9" x 13" pan. Refrigerate until firm; cut into pieces. Store in refrigerator.

Yield: 8 dozen pieces fudge

Glazed Lemon Cheesecake

Glazed Lemon Cheesecake must be made at least 8 hours in advance.

Crust
- 2 1/2 cups graham cracker crumbs
- 10 tablespoons butter or margarine, melted
- 1/4 cup sugar

Filling
- 3 packages (8 ounces each) cream cheese, softened
- 1 1/4 cups sugar
- 4 eggs
- 4 tablespoons fresh lemon juice
- 1 tablespoon grated lemon zest
- 1 teaspoon lemon extract

Glaze
- 3 tablespoons fresh lemon juice
- 1 tablespoon cornstarch
- 1 jar (10 ounces) seedless raspberry jam or preserves

For crust, combine all ingredients in a medium bowl. Press into bottom and 2" up sides of a greased 9" springform pan. Bake at 350° for 5 minutes. Cool completely on a wire rack.

For filling, beat cream cheese and sugar in a large bowl until fluffy. Add eggs, 1 at a time, beating well after each addition. Add remaining ingredients; beat until well blended. Pour filling into crust. Bake at 350° for 50 to 55 minutes or until set in center. Turn off oven. Leaving door slightly open, leave cheesecake in oven 1 hour. Cool completely on a wire rack. Remove sides of pan.

For glaze, stir lemon juice and cornstarch together to make a thin paste. Melt jam in a small saucepan over low heat. Stirring constantly, add cornstarch mixture and cook over medium heat until mixture thickens slightly. Cool to room temperature. Spread glaze evenly over top of cake. Cover and refrigerate 8 hours or overnight.

Yield: about 16 servings

Cherry Sugarplums

- ⅓ cup butter, softened
- ⅓ cup light corn syrup
- 1 teaspoon cherry flavoring
  Liquid red food coloring
- 4 cups confectioners sugar
- 4 ounces candied cherries, halved
- 6 ounces chocolate candy coating
- 4 ounces bittersweet baking chocolate

In a medium bowl, cream butter and corn syrup until fluffy. Stir in cherry flavoring; tint pink. Beating with an electric mixer, gradually add confectioners sugar to butter mixture until too stiff to beat. Stir in remaining sugar. Pour mixture onto a dampened smooth surface. Knead until very smooth and creamy. Using teaspoonfuls of candy mixture, shape balls around cherry halves. Place balls on waxed paper. Lightly cover with waxed paper and allow to dry overnight at room temperature.

In a heavy medium saucepan over low heat, melt candy coating and bittersweet chocolate. Remove chocolate mixture from heat. Placing each ball on a fork and holding over saucepan, spoon chocolate over balls. Place balls on a baking sheet covered with waxed paper. Place in refrigerator to allow chocolate to harden. Store in an airtight container in a cool place.

Yield: about 5½ dozen candies

Glazed Lemon Cheesecake

Cherry Sugarplums

Kiwi Tart

Crust

- 2 cups finely crushed vanilla wafer cookies (about 48 cookies)
- 1/2 cup finely ground pecans
- 1/2 cup butter or margarine, melted

Filling

- 1 cup milk
- 1 cup whipping cream
- 1 package (8 ounces) cream cheese, softened
- 1 vanilla bean, cut in half lengthwise
- 6 egg yolks
- 1 cup sugar
- 2 tablespoons all-purpose flour
- 6 kiwi, peeled and cut into 1/8" slices

Glaze

- 1 teaspoon cornstarch
- 1 teaspoon water
- 3 tablespoons apple jelly

Kiwi Tart

For crust, combine cookie crumbs, pecans, and butter in a medium bowl. Press into bottom and up sides of an 11" tart pan with removable bottom. Bake at 350° for 12 to 15 minutes or until light brown. Cool completely on a wire rack. Remove crust from pan and place an a serving plate.

For filling, combine milk, cream, cream cheese, and vanilla bean in a large saucepan. Stirring constantly, bring to a boil over medium heat; remove from heat. Cover and let stand 15 minutes. Remove vanilla bean and use a sharp knife to scrape black seeds from bean into milk mixture. Return bean to milk mixture.

In a small bowl, whisk egg yolks, sugar, and flour. Add about 1/2 cup milk mixture to egg mixture; stir until well blended. Add egg mixture to milk mixture in saucepan.

Stirring constantly, bring to a boil over medium heat and cook 2 minutes or until thickened. Remove vanilla bean. Pour filling into crust. Cover and refrigerate until well chilled. Arrange kiwi over filling.

For glaze, combine cornstarch and water in a small bowl; stir until smooth. In a small saucepan, melt jelly over medium heat. Whisk cornstarch mixture into jelly and cook until slightly thickened. Brush glaze evenly over kiwi. Loosely cover and store in refrigerator.
Yield: 8 to 10 servings

Date Bars

Crust

- 1 cup firmly packed brown sugar
- 1 cup butter, softened
- 2 cups quick-cooking oats
- 2 cups all-purpose flour
- ½ teaspoon salt
- ½ teaspoon baking soda
- ½ teaspoon vanilla extract

Filling

- 1 cup chopped dates
- 1 cup sugar
- 1 cup water
- ½ cup chopped walnuts
- 1½ tablespoons all-purpose flour

For crust, combine butter and brown sugar until well blended. Stir in oats, flour, salt, soda, and vanilla until well blended; set aside.

For filling, combine all ingredients in a large saucepan. Bring to a boil and boil for 1 minute; remove from heat.

Press half of the crust mixture into a greased 9" x 13" pan. Pour filling over crust; sprinkle remaining crust mixture on top. Bake at 350° for 25 to 30 minutes or until top is lightly browned. Cool completely in pan and cut into squares.

Yield: 42 date bars

Contributed by Norma Bloom Siar

Lemon-Pecan Candy

- 1¾ cups sugar
- 1 cup whipping cream
- 1 cup miniature marshmallows
- 1¼ teaspoons lemon zest
- 1 teaspoon lemon extract
- 1½ cups chopped pecans

In a large microwave-safe bowl, combine sugar and whipping cream. Microwave on high power (100%) 8 to 12 minutes or until mixture reaches soft-ball stage (approximately 234° to 240°). Test about ½ teaspoon mixture in ice water. Mixture will easily form a ball in ice water but will flatten when held in your hand. Without scraping sides, pour candy into another large heat-resistant bowl. Add marshmallows, lemon zest, and lemon extract; beat 3 to 5 minutes or until mixture thickens and begins to lose its gloss. Stir in pecans. Quickly drop teaspoonfuls of candy onto greased waxed paper; cool completely.

Yield: about 3 dozen candies

Lemon-Pecan Candy

Mexican Chocolate Angel Food Cake

Amish Sugar Cookies
and Variations

Mexican Chocolate Angel Food Cake

1³/₄ cups confectioners sugar, divided
1 cup all-purpose flour
¹/₄ cup cocoa
2¹/₄ teaspoons ground cinnamon, divided
1¹/₂ cups egg whites (10 to 12 large eggs)
1¹/₂ teaspoons cream of tartar
1 teaspoon vanilla extract
1 cup granulated sugar
Garnish: sugared grapes

Preheat oven to 350°. In a medium bowl, sift 1¹/₂ cups confectioners sugar, flour, cocoa, and 2 teaspoons cinnamon 3 times.

In a large bowl, beat egg whites, cream of tartar, and vanilla with an electric mixer until soft peaks form, Gradually add granulated sugar, 2 tablespoons at a time, and beat until stiff peaks form.

Sift about one-fourth of confectioners sugar mixture over egg white mixture; fold in gently by hand. Continue to sift and fold in confectioners sugar mixture in small batches. Lightly spoon batter into an ungreased 10" tube pan and place on lower rack of oven. Bake 40 to 45 minutes or until top springs back when lightly touched. Remove from oven and invert pan onto neck of a bottle; cool completely. Remove cake from pan, placing bottom side up on a serving plate.

To decorate, combine remaining ¹/₄ cup confectioners sugar and ¹/₄ teaspoon cinnamon in a small bowl. Place a 10" round paper doily on top of cake and lightly sift confectioners sugar mixture over doily. Carefully remove doily. Garnish, if desired.
Yield: about 12 servings

Amish Sugar Cookies

Variations on basic cookie are listed below.

- 1/2 cup butter or margarine, softened
- 1 1/2 cups sugar
- 1/2 cup sour cream
- 2 eggs
- 1 1/2 teaspoons vanilla extract
- 2 cups all-purpose flour
- 1 teaspoon baking powder
- 1/4 teaspoon salt

In a large bowl, cream butter and sugar until fluffy. Add sour cream, eggs, and vanilla; beat until smooth. In a small bowl, combine flour, baking powder, and salt. Add dry ingredients to creamed mixture; stir until a soft dough forms. Drop teaspoonfuls of dough 2" apart onto a lightly greased baking sheet. Bake at 375° for 8 to 10 minutes or until bottoms are lightly browned. Transfer cookies to a wire rack to cool. Store in an airtight container.
Yield: about 6 1/2 dozen cookies

Chocolate-Chocolate Chip Cookies:

Make Amish Sugar Cookies, adding 2 ounces melted semisweet baking chocolate to butter and sour cream mixture. Add 1 cup semisweet mini chocolate chips to dough.

Cherry-Almond Cookies:

Make Amish Sugar Cookies, using 1 teaspoon almond extract instead of vanilla extract. Add 3/4 cup finely chopped red candied cherries and 3/4 cup finely chopped, toasted slivered almonds to dough.

Lemon-Pecan Cookies:

Make Amish Sugar Cookies, using 1 teaspoon lemon extract instead of vanilla extract. Add 1 cup finely chopped, toasted pecans to dough.

Spice-Walnut Cookies:

Make Amish Sugar Cookies, adding 3/4 teaspoon ground cinnamon and 1/8 teaspoon ground cloves to dry ingredients. Add 1 cup chopped walnuts to dough.

***

Pecan Lace Cookies

- 1 cup finely chopped pecans
- 1/2 cup butter or margarine, softened
- 1/2 cup firmly packed brown sugar
- 2 tablespoons rum, divided
- 2 tablespoons whipping cream
- 1/3 cup semisweet chocolate chips
- 1/4 cup all-purpose flour
- 1/4 teaspoon salt
- 1/8 teaspoon baking soda
- 1 cup quick-cooking oats

Spread pecans evenly on an ungreased baking sheet and bake at 350° for 5 to 8 minutes, stirring once. Remove from oven and cool completely on pan.

In a large bowl, cream butter and sugar until fluffy. Beat in 1 tablespoon rum. In a small saucepan, heat cream over medium heat until boiling. Reduce heat to medium-low. Stir in remaining 1 tablespoon rum and simmer 2 to 3 minutes. Remove from heat; add chocolate chips and stir until smooth. Add chocolate mixture to creamed mixture and stir until well blended. In a medium bowl, sift together next 3 ingredients. Stir dry ingredients into chocolate mixture. Fold in oats and toasted pecans. Drop batter by heaping teaspoonfuls 4" apart onto a greased baking sheet. Use fingers to press each cookie into a 2" diameter circle. Bake at 350° for 8 minutes (cookies will be soft); cool on pan 3 minutes. Transfer to a wire rack to cool completely. Store in an airtight container.
Yield: about 4 dozen cookies

Blueberries & Cream
Cheesecake

Cranberry Sangria
(recipe on page 97)

Blueberries & Cream Cheesecake

Crust

- 1 package (12 ounces) vanilla wafer cookies, finely crushed
- ³/₄ cup butter or margarine, melted

Filling

- 5 packages (8 ounces each) cream cheese, softened
- 1¹/₂ cups sugar
- 6 eggs
- 2 egg yolks
- 3 tablespoons all-purpose flour
- 3 teaspoons vanilla extract
- ¹/₄ cup whipping cream

Topping

- 3 tablespoons cornstarch
- 1 cup plus 3 tablespoons water, divided
- 1 cup sugar
- 1 package (16 ounces) frozen unsweetened blueberries, thawed and drained

For crust, combine cookie crumbs and butter. Press into bottom and halfway up sides of a greased 9" springform pan. Cover and refrigerate.

For filling, beat cream cheese 25 minutes in a large bowl, adding 1 package at a time. Add sugar and beat 5 minutes longer. Add eggs and egg yolks, one at a time, beating 2 minutes after each addition. Beat in flour and vanilla. Beat in cream. Preheat oven to 500°. Pour filling into crust. Bake 10 minutes. Reduce heat to 200°. Bake 1 hour. Turn oven off and leave cheesecake in oven 1 hour without opening door. Cool completely on a wire rack. Remove sides of pan.

For topping, combine cornstarch and 3 tablespoons water in a small bowl; stir until smooth. Combine sugar and remaining 1 cup water in a small saucepan. Stirring constantly, cook over medium heat until sugar dissolves. Stirring constantly, add cornstarch mixture and cook until mixture boils and thickens. Remove from heat and cool to room temperature. Stir in blueberries. Spoon topping over cheesecake. Loosely cover and refrigerate 8 hours or overnight. Serve chilled. **Yield:** about 16 servings

Almond Rocha

    1 pound butter (not
       margarine), at room
       temperature
    2 cups sugar
1½ cups whole shelled
       almonds
    1 teaspoon vanilla extract
    1 package (16 ounces)
       semisweet chocolate
       chips, divided
    3 cups finely chopped
       walnuts, divided

Use a small amount of the butter to grease an 11" x 15" jellyroll pan; set aside.

In a heavy saucepan, place remaining butter and sugar. Cook on high heat 5 minutes, stirring constantly. Attach a candy thermometer to pan. Reduce heat to medium. Add almonds and cook without stirring, until mixture reaches hard-crack stage (approximately 300° to 310°) and turns light golden in color. Test about ½ teaspoon in ice water. Mixture will form brittle threads in ice water and remain brittle when removed from the water. Remove from heat and add vanilla extract. Pour into prepared pan, spreading evenly. Let cool a few minutes; sprinkle 1 cup of chocolate chips on top. Spread the chocolate evenly. Sprinkle with 1½ cups walnuts, pressing nuts into the warm chocolate. Refrigerate until chocolate hardens.

Then, loosen the edges with a knife and turn candy over in pan. Bring to room temperature. Heat remaining 1 cup chocolate chips in the microwave at 1 minute intervals on 50% power, stirring after each minute, until chocolate melts. Spread warm chocolate on candy and sprinkle with remaining walnuts; press nuts into chocolate. Refrigerate until chocolate hardens. Break into pieces.

Yield: about 3½ pounds candy
Contributed by Peggy Wenger

Almond Rocha

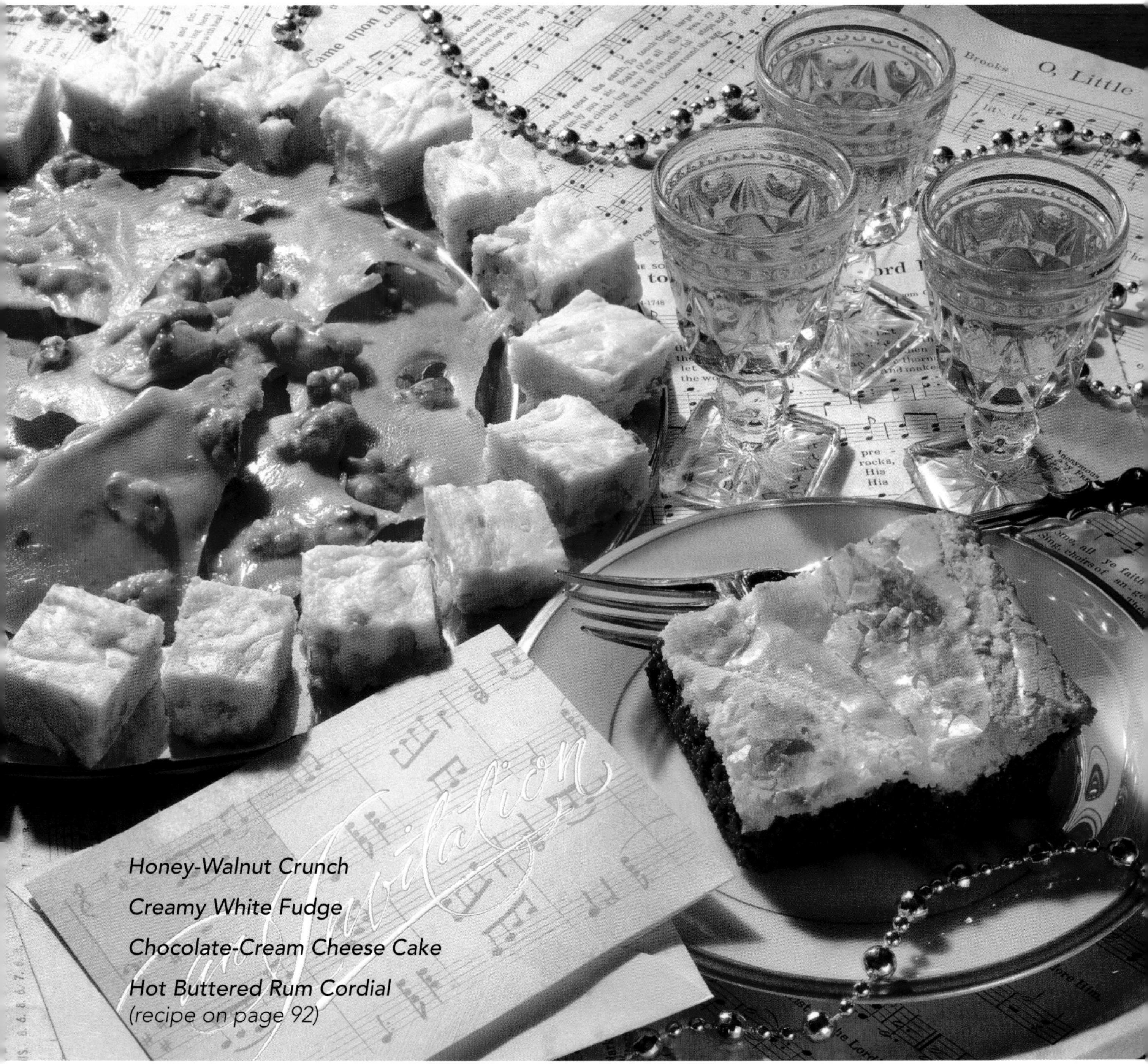

An Invitation

Honey-Walnut Crunch

Creamy White Fudge

Chocolate-Cream Cheese Cake

Hot Buttered Rum Cordial
(recipe on page 92)

Creamy White Fudge

    3   cups sugar
    1   cup sour cream
$1/3$ cup light corn syrup
    2   tablespoons butter or
        margarine
$1/4$ teaspoon salt
    2   teaspoons vanilla extract
    1   cup chopped walnuts

Butter sides of a large heavy saucepan or Dutch oven. Combine sugar, sour cream, corn syrup, butter, and salt in pan. Stirring constantly, cook over medium-low heat until sugar dissolves. Using a pastry brush dipped in hot water, wash down any sugar crystals on sides of pan. Attach candy thermometer to pan, making sure thermometer does not touch bottom of pan. Increase heat to medium and bring to a boil. Cook, without stirring, until syrup reaches soft-ball stage (approximately 234° to 240°). Test about $1/2$ teaspoon syrup in ice water. Syrup should easily form a ball in ice water but flatten when held in your hand. Place pan in 2" of cold water in sink. Add vanilla; do not stir until syrup cools to approximately 200°. Using medium speed of an electric mixer, beat until thickened and no longer glossy. Stir in walnuts. Pour into a buttered 7" x 11" baking pan. Cool completely. Cut into 1" squares. Store in an airtight container in refrigerator.
Yield: about 5 dozen pieces fudge

Honey-Walnut Crunch

$1/2$ cups sugar
$1/2$ cup honey
$1/2$ cup corn syrup
$1/4$ cup water
    1   cup chopped walnuts
    2   tablespoons butter or
        margarine
    1   teaspoon lemon extract
$1/2$ teaspoon salt
$1/2$ teaspoon baking soda

Butter sides of a large heavy saucepan. Combine sugar, honey, corn syrup, and water in pan. Stirring constantly, cook over medium-low heat until sugar dissolves. Using a pastry brush dipped in hot water, wash down any sugar crystals on sides of pan. Attach candy thermometer to pan, making sure thermometer does not touch bottom of pan. Increase heat to medium and bring to a boil. Cook, without stirring, until syrup reaches hard-crack stage (approximately 300° to 310°) and turns light golden in color. Test about $1/2$ teaspoon syrup in ice water. Syrup should form brittle threads in ice water and remain brittle when removed from the water. Remove from heat; stir in walnuts, butter, lemon extract, and salt; stir until butter melts. Add baking soda (mixture will foam); stir until soda dissolves. Pour candy onto a large piece of buttered aluminum foil. Using 2 greased spoons, pull edges of warm candy until stretched thin. Cool completely. Break into pieces. Store in an airtight container.
Yield: about $1^1/_2$ pounds candy

Chocolate-Cream Cheese Cake

    1   package (18.25 ounces)
        devil's food cake mix
        without pudding in the
        mix
    4   eggs, divided
$1/2$ cup butter or margarine,
        softened
$3^1/2$ cups confectioners sugar
    1   package (8 ounces) cream
        cheese, softened

For cake, combine cake mix, 2 eggs, and butter in a large bowl; beat 2 minutes. Spread batter in a greased and floured 9" x 13" glass baking dish. In a small bowl, beat remaining 2 eggs, sugar, and cream cheese until smooth. Spread over cake batter. Bake at 350° for 35 to 40 minutes or until cake begins to pull away from sides of pan. Cool completely on a wire rack. Store in an airtight container.
Yield: about 12 servings

Lady Baltimore Cake

Fruit Filling
- 1 cup chopped dried figs
- 1/2 cup chopped golden raisins
- 1/2 cup orange juice

Cake
- 1 cup butter or margarine, softened
- 2 cups sugar
- 1 teaspoon grated orange zest
- 3 cups sifted cake flour
- 1 tablespoon baking powder
- 1/4 teaspoon salt
- 1/2 cup orange juice
- 1/2 cup water
- 2 teaspoons vanilla extract
- 8 egg whites

Icing
- 1 1/2 cups sugar
- 5 tablespoons water
- 2 egg whites
- 2 tablespoons light corn syrup
- 1/4 teaspoon cream of tartar
- 1 teaspoon vanilla extract
- 1 cup chopped pecans

For fruit filling, combine figs, raisins, and orange juice in a small bowl; set aside.

For cake, grease three 9" round cake pans. Line bottom of pans with waxed paper; grease waxed paper. In a large bowl, cream butter, sugar, and orange zest. In a medium bowl, combine cake flour, baking powder, and salt. In a small bowl, combine orange juice, water, and vanilla. Alternately add dry ingredients and orange juice mixture to creamed mixture, beating until well blended. In a medium bowl, beat egg whites until stiff peaks form. Fold egg whites into batter; pour into prepared pans. Bake at 350° for 20 to 25 minutes or until a toothpick inserted in center of cake comes out clean. Cool in pans 10 minutes. Remove from pans and cool completely on a wire rack.

For icing, drain fruit mixture; set aside. In top of a double boiler, combine sugar, water, egg whites, corn syrup, and cream of tartar. Beat with an electric mixer until sugar is well blended. Place over simmering water; beat about 7 minutes or until soft peaks form. Remove from heat and add vanilla. Continue beating 2 minutes longer or until icing is desired consistency. In a medium bowl, fold fruit mixture and pecans into 1 cup icing. Spread filling between layers. Ice top and sides of cake with remaining icing. Store in an airtight container in refrigerator.
Yield: about 12 servings

Lady Baltimore Cake

Heavenly Angel Cookies

Heavenly Angel Cookies

Cookies

- ³/₄ cup butter or margarine, softened
- 1 package (3 ounces) cream cheese, softened
- 1³/₄ cups confectioners sugar
- 1 egg
- ¹/₂ teaspoon vanilla extract
- ¹/₂ teaspoon almond extract
- 2 cups all-purpose flour
- ³/₄ teaspoon baking powder

Icing

- 3 cups confectioners sugar
- 2¹/₂ to 3 tablespoons water
- 2 teaspoons light corn syrup
- ¹/₂ teaspoon vanilla extract
- Pink paste food coloring

For cookies, cream butter, cream cheese, and confectioners sugar in a large bowl. Beat in egg and extracts. In a small bowl, combine flour and baking powder. Add dry ingredients to creamed mixture; stir until a soft dough forms. Divide dough into fourths. Wrap in plastic wrap and chill 2 hours or until firm enough to handle.

On a lightly floured surface, use a floured rolling pin to roll out one fourth of dough to ¹/₈" thickness. Use a 4"w x 4¹/₄"h angel-shaped cookie cutter to cut out cookies. Transfer to an ungreased baking sheet.

Bake at 350° for 7 to 9 minutes or until bottoms are lightly browned. Transfer cookies to a wire rack to cool.

For icing, combine confectioners sugar, water, corn syrup, and vanilla in a medium bowl; tint light pink. Spoon icing into a pastry bag fitted with a small round tip. Pipe hair, face, and wing design onto each cookie. Use a medium tip to outline and fill in dresses with icing. Allow icing to harden. Store in a single layer in an airtight container.

Yield: about 1¹/₂ dozen cookies

Peppermint Stocking Cookies

Cookies

3¹/₄ cups all-purpose flour
1 tablespoon baking powder
¹/₂ cup butter or margarine, softened
1¹/₄ cups granulated sugar
1 egg
2¹/₂ teaspoons peppermint extract
1 teaspoon vanilla extract
¹/₄ cup milk

Icing

1 cup confectioners sugar
1 tablespoon butter, softened
2 tablespoons milk
Red paste food coloring

In a medium mixing bowl, combine flour and baking powder. In a large mixing bowl, cream butter, sugar, egg, and extracts. Add the dry ingredients alternately with milk. On a lightly floured surface, use a floured rolling pin to roll out dough to ¹/₈" thickness. Using a 3" high stocking cookie cutter, cut out dough. Transfer cookies to a lightly greased baking sheet. Bake at 350° for 8 to 10 minutes or until edges are lightly browned. Remove from pan and cool on wire racks.

For icing, beat together sugar, butter, and milk until smooth. Stir in food coloring. Ice cookies at the stocking cuff, heel, and toe.

Yield: about 3 dozen 3" cookies

Fudge Meltaways

³/₄ cup butter or margarine, divided
3 ounces unsweetened baking chocolate, chopped and divided
1¹/₂ cups finely crushed vanilla wafer cookies
1 cup sweetened shredded coconut
¹/₂ cup chopped pecans
¹/₄ cup granulated sugar
1 egg
2 teaspoons vanilla extract, divided
2 cups confectioners sugar
3 tablespoons milk

Stirring constantly, melt ¹/₂ cup butter and 1 ounce chocolate in a large saucepan over low heat. Remove from heat; stir in next 5 ingredients and 1 teaspoon vanilla. Press into a buttered 7" x 11" baking pan. Bake at 350° for 8 minutes. Cool completely.

Stirring constantly, melt remaining ¹/₄ cup butter and 2 ounces chocolate in a medium saucepan over low heat. Remove from heat; stir in confectioners sugar, milk, and remaining 1 teaspoon vanilla. Spread over crumb mixture in pan. Cool completely. Cut into 1" squares.

Yield: about 5 dozen candies

Microwave Caramel Corn

Vegetable cooking spray
16 cups popped popcorn
1 cup firmly packed brown sugar
2 tablespoons light corn syrup
2 tablespoons molasses
¹/₂ teaspoon salt
¹/₂ teaspoon baking soda
¹/₂ teaspoon vanilla extract

Spray inside of a 14" x 20" oven cooking bag with cooking spray. Place popcorn in bag. In a 2-quart microwave-safe bowl, combine next 3 ingredients. Microwave on high power (100%) 2 minutes or until mixture boils. Stir and microwave on high power 2 minutes longer. Stir in remaining ingredients. Pour syrup over popcorn; stir and shake until well coated (mixture will be hot). Microwave on high power 1¹/₂ minutes. Stir, shake, and microwave 1¹/₂ minutes longer. Spread on aluminum foil sprayed with cooking spray. Cool completely. Store in an airtight container.

Yield: about 16 cups caramel corn

Sesame Candy

1 cup sesame seeds, divided
1 cup old-fashioned oats
1 cup confectioners sugar
3/4 cup nonfat dry milk
3/4 cup smooth peanut butter
1/2 cup honey
2 tablespoons water
1 teaspoon vanilla extract

Spread sesame seeds on an ungreased baking sheet. Bake at 350° for 5 to 8 minutes or until light brown. Cool completely on pan.

In a medium bowl, combine 1/4 cup sesame seeds and remaining ingredients, stirring until well blended. Shape into 1" balls. Roll in remaining 3/4 cup sesame seeds. Cover and refrigerate.
Yield: about 6 dozen candies

Sesame Candy
Fudge Meltaways
Microwave Caramel Corn

Cinnamon-Chocolate Stars

Cookies

- 1 cup butter or margarine, softened
- $3/4$ cup granulated sugar
- 1 egg
- 1 teaspoon vanilla extract
- 1 package (6 ounces) semisweet chocolate chips, melted
- 3 cups all-purpose flour
- $1/2$ teaspoon ground cinnamon
- $1/4$ teaspoon salt

Icing

- $2 1/4$ cups confectioners sugar
- 6 tablespoons milk

For cookies, cream butter and sugar until fluffy in a large bowl. Add egg and vanilla; beat until smooth. Stir in chocolate. In a medium bowl, sift together flour, cinnamon, and salt. Add dry ingredients to chocolate mixture; knead in bowl until a soft dough forms, On a lightly floured surface, use a floured rolling pin to roll out dough to $1/4$" thickness. Use $1 1/2$" and $2 1/2$" star-shaped cookie cutters to cut out cookies. Transfer to a greased baking sheet. Bake at 300° for 15 to 20 minutes or until firm. Transfer to a wire rack to cool completely.

For icing, stir sugar and milk together in a medium bowl until smooth. Spread icing on cookies; allow icing to harden. Store in an airtight container.
Yield: about 7 dozen cookies

Belgian Nut Cookies

- $3/4$ cup butter, softened
- $1/3$ cup sugar
- $1 1/2$ cups all-purpose flour
- $1 1/2$ cups toasted ground almonds
- 1 teaspoon vanilla extract
- $1/8$ teaspoon salt
- 1 cup semisweet chocolate chips
- $1/2$ cup raspberry jam

In a large mixing bowl, cream butter and sugar. Add flour, almonds, vanilla, and salt stirring just until mixture is combined and forms a dough. Divide dough in half and wrap each half in plastic wrap. Refrigerate 1 hour.

Roll out dough to $1/8$" thickness between two sheets of waxed paper. Remove top sheet of waxed paper. Using a $2 1/2$" long fluted tart mold or cookie cutter, cut out dough. Place cookies on lightly greased baking sheet. Bake at 350° for 10 to 12 minutes or until lightly browned around edges. Cool cookies on baking sheet.

In the top of a double boiler over low heat, melt chocolate chips. Reserving $1/4$ cup of melted chocolate, spread a thin layer of chocolate on $1/2$ of the total cookies. Spread the remaining cookies with a thin layer of raspberry jam. With one chocolate side and one raspberry side together, place two cookies together. Place cookies on waxed paper-lined baking sheet. Drizzle tops of cookies with reserved chocolate. Place cookies in refrigerator to allow chocolate to harden. Store cookies in airtight container in cool, dry place.
Yield: about 2 dozen cookies

helpful how-tos

Knit

Abbreviations

cm	centimeters
K	knit
mm	millimeters
P	purl
st(s)	stitch(es)

( ) or [ ] — work all instructions **as many** times as specified by the number immediately following **or** contains explanatory remarks.

Gauge

Exact gauge is essential for proper size. Before beginning your project, make a sample swatch in the yarn and needle specified in the instructions. After completing the swatch, measure it, counting your stitches and rows carefully. If your swatch is larger or smaller than specified, make another, changing needle size to get the correct gauge. Keep trying until you find the size needles that will give you the specified gauge.

Weaving Seams

With the **right** side of both pieces facing you and edges even, sew through both sides once to secure the seam. Insert the needle under the bar **between** the first and second stitches on the row and pull the yarn through (Fig. 1). Insert the needle under the next bar on the second side. Repeat from side to side, being careful to match rows.

Fig. 1

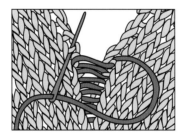

Tassel

Cut a piece of cardboard 3" (7.5 cm) wide and as long as the finished tassel. Wind a double strand of yarn around the cardboard about 12 times. Cut an 18" (45.5 cm) length of yarn and insert it under all of the strands at the top of the cardboard; pull up **tightly** and tie securely; leave the ends long. Cut the yarn at the opposite end of the cardboard and remove it (Fig. 2a). Cut a 6" (15 cm) length of yarn and wrap it **tightly** around the tassel twice, 1" (2.5 cm) below the top (Fig. 2b); tie securely and trim the ends.

Fig. 2a

Fig. 2b

Pom-Pom

Cut a piece of cardboard 3"
(7.5 cm) wide and as long as the
diameter of the pom-pom.
Wind the yarn around the
cardboard until it is about ¹/₂"
(12 mm) thick in the middle
(Fig. 3a).
Carefully slip the yarn off the
cardboard and firmly tie an 18"
(45.5 cm) length of yarn around the
middle (Fig. 3b). Leave the yarn
ends long enough to attach the
pom-pom. Cut the loops on both
ends and trim the pom-pom into a
smooth ball (Fig. 3c).

Fig. 3a

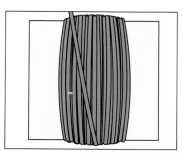

Fig. 3b

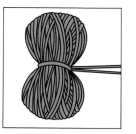

Fig. 3c

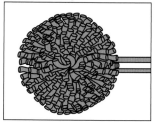

Embroidery Stitches

Follow the stitch diagrams to bring the needle
up at odd numbers and down at even numbers.

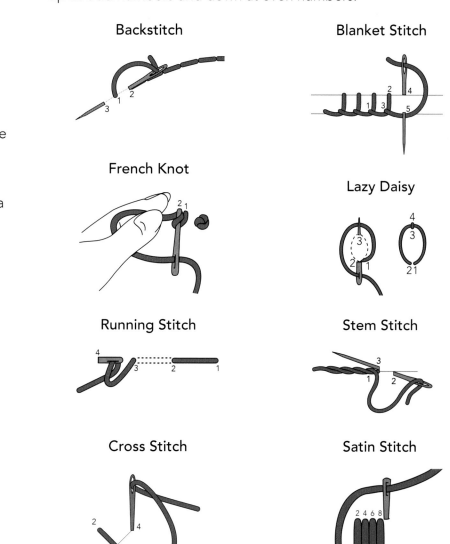

Backstitch

Blanket Stitch

French Knot

Lazy Daisy

Running Stitch

Stem Stitch

Cross Stitch

Satin Stitch

Straight Stitch

Sizing Patterns

To change the size of a pattern, divide the desired height or width of the pattern (whichever is larger) by the actual height or width of the pattern. Multiply the result by 100 and photocopy the pattern at this percentage.

For example: You want your pattern to be 8" high, but the pattern on the page is 6" high. So 8 ÷ 6 = 1.33 x 100 = 133%. Copy the pattern at 133%.

Making Patterns

When the entire pattern is shown, place tracing paper over the pattern and draw over the lines.

When only half or a quarter of the pattern is shown (indicated by a solid blue line or solid gold line on the pattern), trace the pattern half or quarter. Fold the fabric in half or quarters and match the fold markings of the pattern to the fabric folds.

Transferring Patterns

Pick the transfer method that works best with the fabric and project you've chosen. If you choose the water-soluble pen method, check first on a scrap piece to make sure the floss won't bleed when you remove the pen markings.

Tissue Paper Method

Trace the pattern onto tissue paper. Pin the tissue paper to the fabric and stitch through the paper. Carefully tear the tissue paper away.

Water-Soluble Marking Pen Method

Trace the pattern onto tracing paper. Tape the traced pattern and fabric to a sunny window; then, trace the pattern onto the fabric with the pen. Embroider the design. Lightly spritz the finished design with water to remove any visible pen markings.

Using Jump Rings

To open a jump ring, use two pairs of needle-nose jewelry pliers to grasp the ring near each side of the opening. Pull one set of pliers toward you and push the other away to open the ring (Fig. 4). Move the pliers the opposite way to close the ring. (**Note:** *Opening a jump ring by pulling the ends away from each other will weaken and distort the ring.*)

Making Eye Loops

Grasp the end of a wire length or head pin with round-nose jewelry pliers (Fig. 5a). Repositioning the pliers as needed, bend the wire end into a small loop (Fig. 5b). Cut off any excess wire (Fig. 5c). To open an eye loop, follow the instructions for opening a jump ring.

Adding Crimp Beads

String a crimp bead on the wire. Place the bead on the inner groove of the crimping tool and squeeze (Fig. 6a). Open the tool, turn the bead a quarter turn and place it in the outer groove of the tool. Squeeze to round out the bead (Fig. 6b).

Fig. 4

Fig. 5a   Fig. 5b

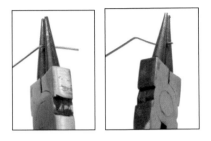

Fig. 5c

Fig. 6a

Fig. 6b

Stem Stitch

French Knot

Lazy Daisy

Sunbonnet Sue Apron
from page 13
enlarge to 109%

Happy Gift Tag
from page 35

happy
christmas

Leisure Arts, Inc., grants permission to the owner of this book to photocopy the patterns on pages 143-158 for personal use only.

Daily Kitchen Towels
from page 14
enlarge all patterns to 162%

- = = = Running Stitch
- ///// Stem Stitch
- •• French Knot
- ◊◊ Lazy Daisy
- / Straight Stitch

- - - - Running Stitch
- ///// Stem Stitch
- ••• French Knot
- / Straight Stitch

monday

TUESDAY

SUNDAY

- = = = Running Stitch
- ///// Stem Stitch
- ••• French Knot
- ◊ Lazy Daisy
- / Straight Stitch

- - - Running Stitch

///// Stem Stitch

• • • French Knot

═ ═ ═ Running Stitch

///// Stem Stitch

• • French Knot

◯ Lazy Daisy

∣ Straight Stitch

WEDNESDAY

THURSDAY

SATURDAY

═ ═ ═ Running Stitch

///// Stem Stitch

• • French Knot

- - - Running Stitch

// Stem Stitch

• French Knot

/// Backstitch

FRIDAY

...And to all a Good Night

/ Backstitch
● French Knot
◗ Lazy Daisy

Border

Bluebird
from page 15
enlarge to 184%

Stem Stitch

Running Stitch

Garnet
Pillow
from page 14
enlarge to fit
your pillow

𝒫 Lazy Daisy   ╱ Straight Stitch   ■ Satin Stitch   · French Knot (wrapped twice)

╱╱╱ Stem Stitch   – – – Running Stitch   ● French Knot (wrapped 4 times)

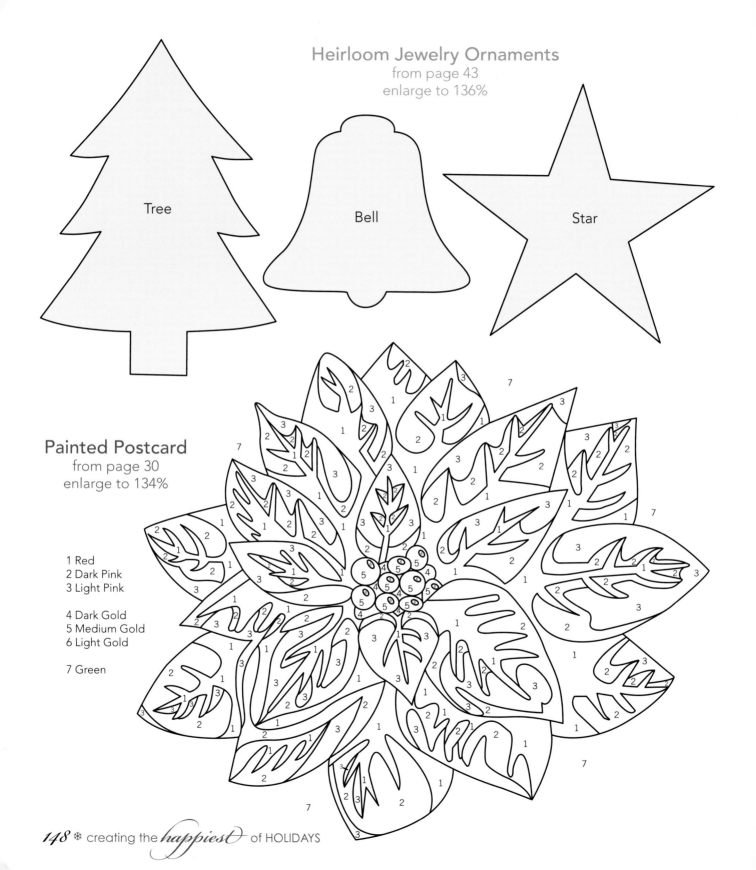

Heirloom Jewelry Ornaments
from page 43
enlarge to 136%

Tree

Bell

Star

Painted Postcard
from page 30
enlarge to 134%

1 Red
2 Dark Pink
3 Light Pink

4 Dark Gold
5 Medium Gold
6 Light Gold

7 Green

Embroidered Card
from page 29

Petal

Fabric Mini Gift Bags
from page 38

Nativity Silhouette Card
from page 29

patterns ❋ *149*

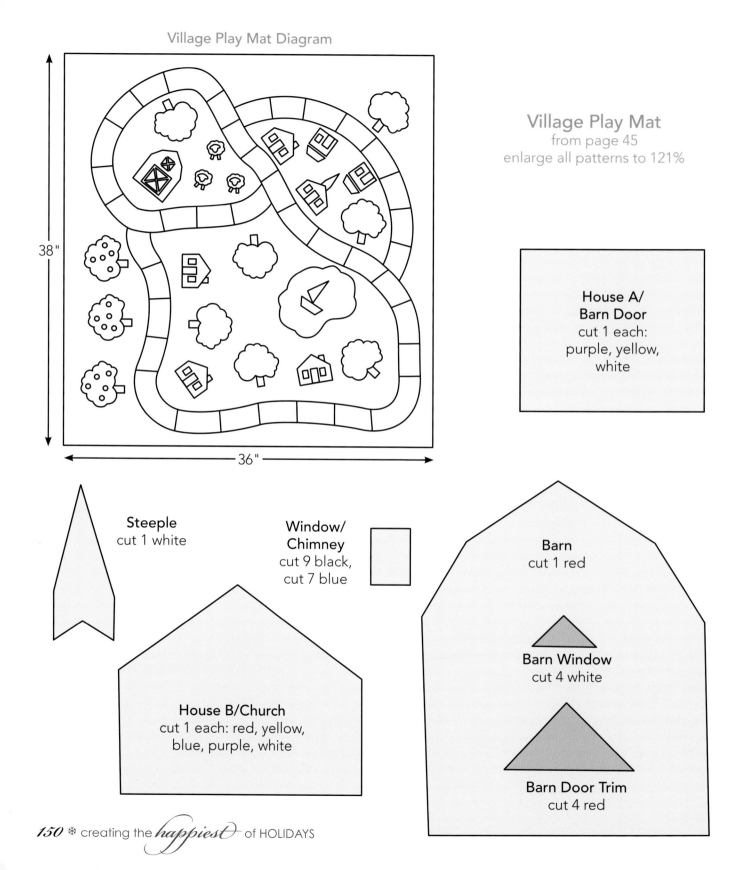

Village Play Mat Diagram

38"

36"

Village Play Mat
from page 45
enlarge all patterns to 121%

House A/
Barn Door
cut 1 each:
purple, yellow,
white

Steeple
cut 1 white

Window/
Chimney
cut 9 black,
cut 7 blue

Barn
cut 1 red

Barn Window
cut 4 white

Barn Door Trim
cut 4 red

House B/Church
cut 1 each: red, yellow,
blue, purple, white

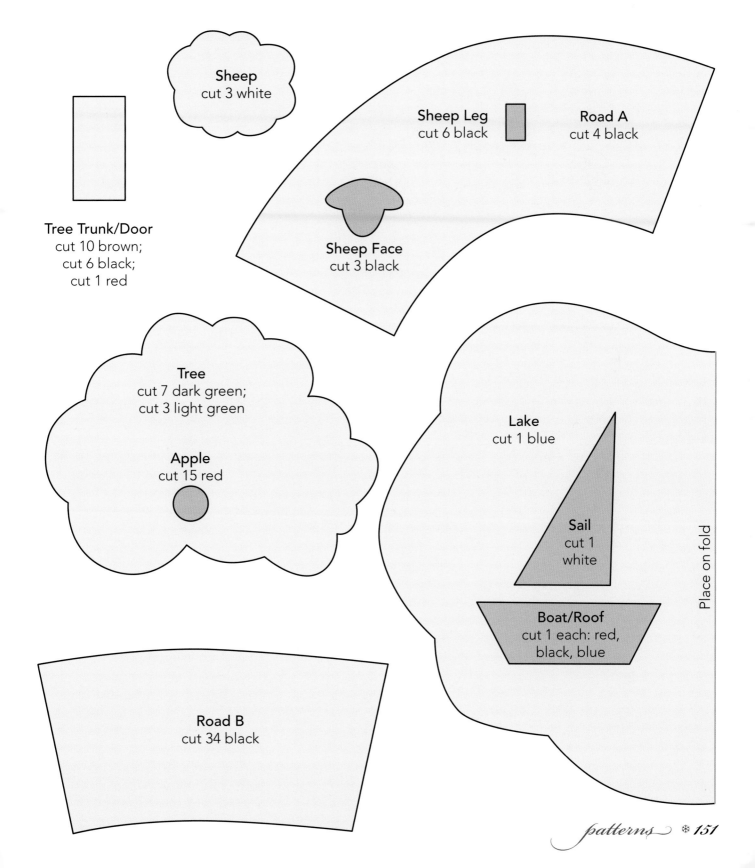

Sheep
cut 3 white

Sheep Leg
cut 6 black

Road A
cut 4 black

Sheep Face
cut 3 black

Tree Trunk/Door
cut 10 brown;
cut 6 black;
cut 1 red

Tree
cut 7 dark green;
cut 3 light green

Apple
cut 15 red

Lake
cut 1 blue

Sail
cut 1
white

Boat/Roof
cut 1 each: red,
black, blue

Place on fold

Road B
cut 34 black

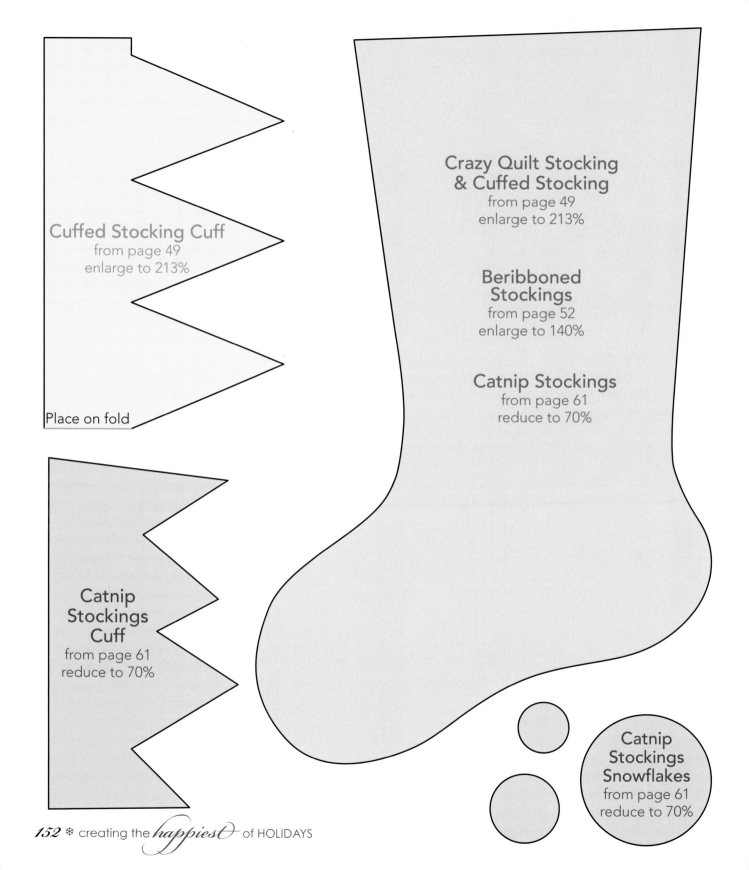

Cuffed Stocking Cuff
from page 49
enlarge to 213%

Place on fold

Catnip
Stockings
Cuff
from page 61
reduce to 70%

Crazy Quilt Stocking
& Cuffed Stocking
from page 49
enlarge to 213%

Beribboned
Stockings
from page 52
enlarge to 140%

Catnip Stockings
from page 61
reduce to 70%

Catnip
Stockings
Snowflakes
from page 61
reduce to 70%

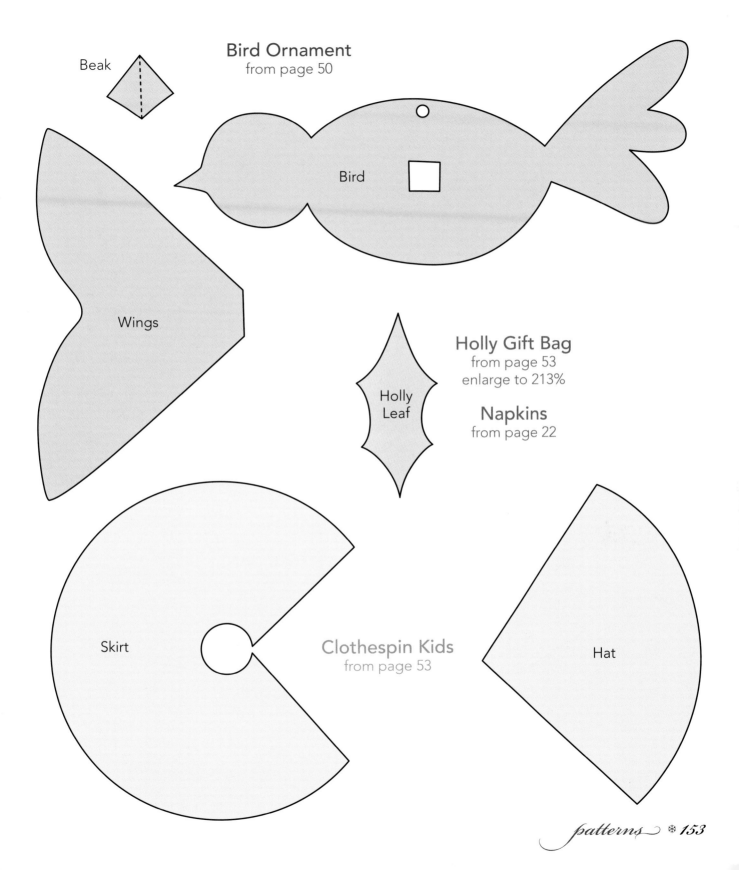

Beak

Bird Ornament
from page 50

Bird

Wings

Holly Gift Bag
from page 53
enlarge to 213%

Napkins
from page 22

Holly
Leaf

Skirt

Clothespin Kids
from page 53

Hat

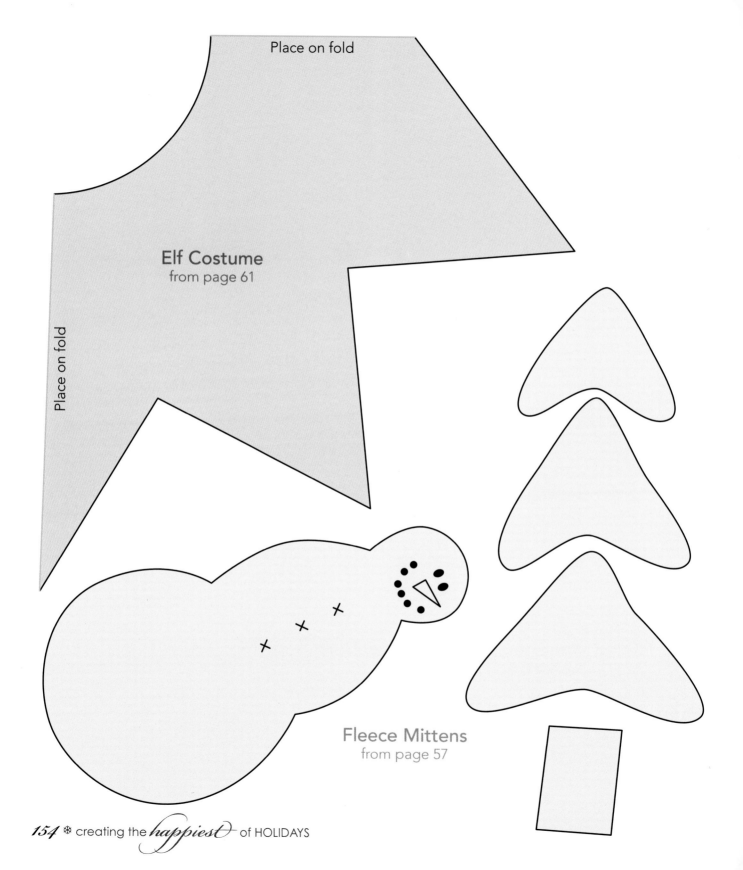

Place on fold

Elf Costume
from page 61

Place on fold

Fleece Mittens
from page 57

Santa Stepping Stone
from page 56
enlarge to 161%

Etched Nativity Shade
from page 56

**Home Sweet Home
Mug & Mat**
from page 56

Joy Tin
from page 79

Christmas Tree Gift Bags
from page 72

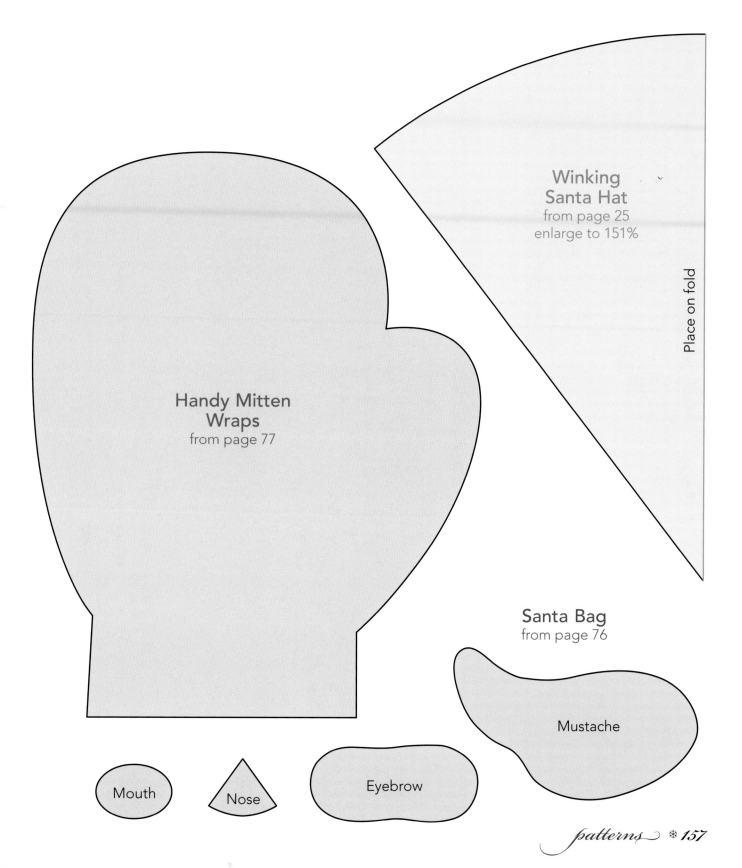

Winking
Santa Hat
from page 25
enlarge to 151%

Place on fold

Handy Mitten
Wraps
from page 77

Santa Bag
from page 76

Mustache

Mouth

Nose

Eyebrow

Fruited Rice Mix
from page 73

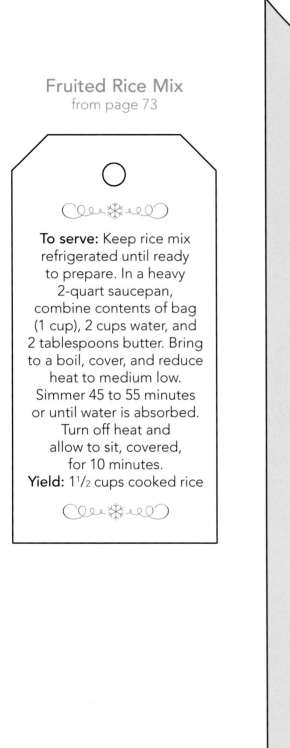

To serve: Keep rice mix refrigerated until ready to prepare. In a heavy 2-quart saucepan, combine contents of bag (1 cup), 2 cups water, and 2 tablespoons butter. Bring to a boil, cover, and reduce heat to medium low. Simmer 45 to 55 minutes or until water is absorbed. Turn off heat and allow to sit, covered, for 10 minutes. **Yield:** 1½ cups cooked rice

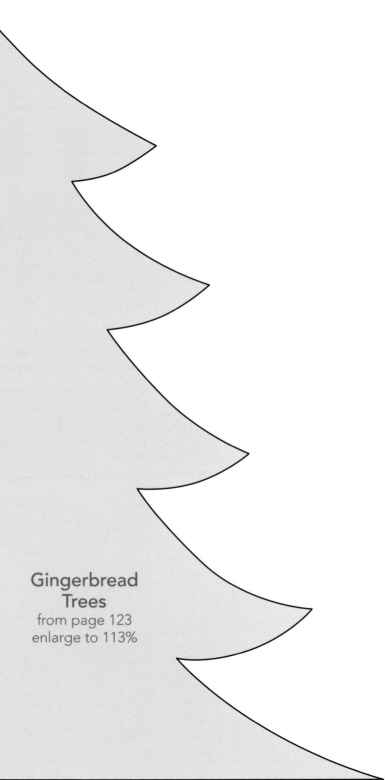

Gingerbread Trees
from page 123
enlarge to 113%

Project Index

Recipe Index